LEGENDS

THE ULTIMATE GUIDE TO THE SPORT'S LEGENDARY DRIVERS

igloobooks

igloobooks

Published in 2016
by Igloo Books Ltd
Cottage Farm
Sywell
NN6 0BJ
www.igloobooks.com

Cover images © tl Xinhua/Alamy Stock Photo;
tr GP Library Limited/Alamy Stock Photo; bl Paul Gilham/Getty Images;
bc Tom Gandolfini/AFP/Getty Images; br GP Library Limited/Alamy Stock Photo

Cover designed by Nicholas Gage
Edited by Natalie Baker

Written by Matt Anniss

LEO002 0716
2 4 6 8 10 9 7 5 3 1
ISBN 978-1-78557-829-8

Printed and manufactured in China

CONTENTS

FORMULA 1

It isn't hard to capture the essence of Formula 1. Stripped back to the raw essentials, this motor sport is a gladiatorial contest that pits the world's most talented drivers against each other in gruelling tests of endurance, tactics, fitness, nerve and reflexes. To spice up things further, Formula 1 drivers are racing in some of the most technically advanced cars available – super-fast, aerodynamic beasts that require vast teams of engineers and billions of pounds to develop – at speeds in excess of 186 mph (300 kph). There's an element of danger that intensifies the experience.

While Formula 1 has always been about cars, from the souped-up production sports cars of the 1950s to today's futuristic, scientifically designed super-cars, it's the feats of the drivers that have made the sport what it is today. Unlikely wins, dominant performances, bitter feuds, off-track friendships and on-track rivalries have all helped to turn Formula 1 into an ongoing soap opera on wheels, often with storylines straight out of Hollywood movies.

When motor sport's governing body, the FIA, introduced the Formula 1 category for Grand Prix racing in the late 1940s, it couldn't have predicted just how popular Formula 1 would become. Through decades of thrilling rivalries and seat-of-the-pants racing, Formula 1 has become a sport rich with thrilling stories and tragic tales.

Thanks to seven decades of action-packed history, Formula 1 is blessed with a huge number of legends. These are the drivers whose daring, dangerous exploits have thrilled the world. It's these on-track heroes, a mixture of boy-racers come good, international playboys, fierce competitors, unlikely superstars and intense mavericks, who are celebrated in this book.

Alongside legendary multiple world Champions such as Alain Prost, Michael Schumacher and Sebastian Vettel, you'll also find nearly-men, track stalwarts and those whose careers were tragically ended before they hit their prime. This is the story of Formula 1, as told through the careers of its finest exponents.

Formula 1 is famous for amazing feats of driving, such as Gilles Villeneuve's daring overtaking move at the 1979 Dutch Grand Prix, which saw him move up from fifth place on the grid to lead the race.

The history of Formula 1 is one of innovation. This 1977 Elf Renault RS01, driven by Jean-Pierre Jabouille, boasted the first regularly turbo charged 1.5 litre V6 engine in Formula 1 history.

1950s

GUISEPPI FARINA

The passionate and temperamental Farina was all smiles after taking the chequered flag at Silverstone in May 1950, thereby ensuring his place in Formula 1 history.

Like so many of Formula 1's earliest heroes, Guiseppi Farina (popularly known as "Nino") was a throwback to the early days of Grand Prix racing in the 1930s. By the time he won the inaugural race of the FIA Formula 1 World Championship at Silverstone, England, on 13th May 1950, he had been racing for nearly 20 years.

Farina would guarantee immortality not only by winning that race in front of 200,000 spectators but also by winning the first ever Drivers Championship. By 1950, Farina was already one of the world's most celebrated drivers, having won a trio of Italian championships: 1937, 1938 and 1939. The Italian championship was one of the most competitive on the European circuit at the time as a result of the dominance of Italian-made sports cars. Farina was also a familiar face at Grand Prix around the world, having built up a reputation as a fearless, though some would say reckless, driver-for-hire in an era when private entries outnumbered cars from manufacturers' teams.

Farina first got a taste for racing in his native Italy in the early 1930s. Despite crashing in his first race, he soon became a firm fixture on the Italian circuit-racing scene.

He became renowned for crashing but somehow he survived each accident and kept coming back for more. The great Enzo Ferrari, founder of the Ferrari racing team and a former Grand Prix driver, famously said that Farina "drove as if the devil were behind him and the angels ahead". Farina cheated death on several occasions, invariably blaming his cars rather than his own risky driving style for the high-speed crashes.

Despite regular fall-outs with manufacturers and a history of crashes, Farina became one of the most successful drivers in the world in the years following the Second World War. His frequent podium finishes earned him a spot on the coveted Alfa Romeo team for the inaugural FIA Formula 1 World Championship in 1950.

Farina may have been lucky to be driving the fastest car on the grid at Silverstone, but he made great use of his Alfa 158 to wow the crowds and win the first Formula 1 World Championship race.

STATISTICS

BORN	30th October 1906
NATIONALITY	Italian
ACTIVE YEARS	1950–55
TEAMS	Alfa Romeo, Ferrari
TOTAL RACES	34 (33 starts)
WINS	5
PODIUM FINISHES	20
POLE POSITIONS	5
FIRST WIN	1950 British Grand Prix
LAST WIN	1953 German Grand Prix
LAST RACE	1955 Italian Grand Prix

"Nino" Farina (centre) was demanding of mechanics and had a reputation for blaming them, rather than his own mistakes, for his many crashes.

Farina had the perfect start to the 1950 season, winning the British Grand Prix at Silverstone. He won again in Switzerland three weeks later, and by the penultimate race of the season, he was vying with dashing teammate Juan Manuel Fangio for the World Championship title.

When Fangio qualified fastest for the final race of the season – the Italian Grand Prix at Monza – few gave Farina much hope of finishing ahead of the acclaimed Argentine. However, the Italian produced an inspired performance, taking the lead early. Fangio was forced to retire when his car developed engine problems midway through the race, leaving Farina clear to cruise home for the win that secured the inaugural FIA Formula 1 World Championship.

Sadly, Farina never tasted World Championship success again. He struggled in 1951, with a single win at Spa-Francorchamps in Belgium his only reason to celebrate. A move to the Ferrari team in 1952 saw things go from bad to worse, and it wasn't until the German Grand Prix in 1953 that he finally won again. It would be his last trip to the top step of the podium.

Inevitably, it was a crash that led to Farina's retirement from Formula 1. He missed most of the 1954 season after receiving severe burns during a sports car race at Monza. Although he returned to Formula 1 in 1955, his comeback didn't last long. To cope with the pain he endured while driving, he would regularly dose himself on morphine and amphetamines. In the end, it all became too much and he retired after the Italian Grand Prix in September, a race he didn't even start.

Given his history of crashes, there was a sad inevitability about Farina's death in June 1966. He was killed in a car crash while on his way to the French Grand Prix. He was 59 years old. It was a tragic end to an extraordinary life and career.

ALBERTO
ASCARI

Alberto Ascari celebrates winning the 1952 British Grand Prix at Silverstone, one of six consecutive race victories in his first World Championship winning season.

Alberto Ascari was born to race. He spent his formative years watching his father, Antonio, dominating the European Grand Prix circuit in the early 1920s. Despite his father's death in a crash at the French Grand Prix in 1924, as soon as he was old enough, Alberto took to the track, racing motorbikes rather than cars.

Following the end of the Second World War, Enzo Ferrari invited him to turn his attention to Formula 1 cars. He joined the Italian team in 1949, leading them in the inaugural 1950 World Championship.

Ascari had a disappointing first season, finishing fifth. This changed in 1951, when he pushed his great rival, Argentine hero Juan Manuel Fangio, all the way. A change in the rules, brought on by rising costs and the withdrawal of many teams as a result of arguments over engine size, made Ascari the clear favourite in 1952. With Fangio out of action after breaking his neck in a race at Monza, the Italian dominated the season, winning six of the eight races to claim his first World Championship crown.

Ascari defended his title in 1953, in spite of the return of his Argentine rival. He won five Grand Prix that year, including the first three.

STATISTICS

BORN	13th July 1918
NATIONALITY	Italian
ACTIVE YEARS	1950–55
TEAMS	Ferrari, Maserati, Lancia
TOTAL RACES	33 (32 starts)
WINS	13
PODIUM FINISHES	17
POLE POSITIONS	14
FIRST WIN	1951 German Grand Prix
LAST WIN	1953 Swiss Grand Prix
LAST RACE	1955 Monaco Grand Prix

Ascari's Formula 2 class Ferrari 500 was the dominant car in both the 1952 and 1953 Formula 1 seasons.

Things began to unravel for Ascari in 1954. He'd joined Lancia in a big-money switch, but the car wasn't ready. When it finally arrived in 1955, disaster struck. First, Ascari was lucky to escape alive when he crashed his Lancia into the harbour during the Monaco Grand Prix. Then, just four days later, he was killed in a high-speed crash while testing a Ferrari at Monza.

His death was treated as a national tragedy in Italy, with more than one million people lining the streets of Milan for his funeral. Gianni Lancia, head of the Lancia team, was unable to cope with the grief of the loss of his great friend and wound up his Formula 1 team shortly afterwards.

Alberto Ascari was at his best when leading from the front. Once he was at the front of the field, the Italian was almost impossible to pass.

JUAN MANUEL FANGIO

In his day, Juan Manuel Fangio was every bit as dominant as later Formula 1 legends Michael Schumacher and Sebastian Vettel. Watching him celebrate wins became a regular spectacle at Grand Prix during the 1950s.

Juan Manuel Fangio was Formula 1's first genuine superstar. In an era dominated by nationalist fervour, he was the pride of Argentina. His entrance into European Grand Prix racing in 1949 was paid for by President Juan Perón. It was a smart move by the dictator, as Fangio would go on to dominate Formula 1 during the 1950s, winning five World Championship titles – a record that would stand until Michael Schumacher claimed his sixth crown in 2003.

In many ways, Fangio was ahead of his time. Such was his desire to win that he sought out the fastest cars, regularly switching between teams in order to ensure the greatest chance of success. He won World Championships with four different teams, and once switched teams mid-season. His 1954 title was won in both Maserati and Mercedes cars.

Unlike many of his rivals, whose driving style was fast and erratic, Fangio used to boast of driving at the slowest speed necessary to win. He was mentally tough, incredibly fit – despite being in his 40s during the peak of his career – and tactically astute. He was a professional in an era of enthusiastic amateurs and temperamental speed freaks.

The son of an Italian immigrant, Fangio had his first taste of racing as a ride-on mechanic in a car driven by a customer of the garage where he worked. He soon began to take part in long, gruelling road races and had built up quite a reputation in Argentina by the time racing was suspended following the outbreak of the Second World War.

In 1947, he was invited to race one of two Maserati cars owned by a local racing club against two touring Italian drivers. It spiked his interest in the growing European Grand Prix scene and a move to the continent followed two years later.

Fangio's driving style was controlled and never excessively fast, but his skills were such that he regularly left rivals in his wake.

STATISTICS

BORN	24th June 1911
NATIONALITY	Argentinian
ACTIVE YEARS	1950–58
TEAMS	Alfa Romeo, Maserati, Mercedes, Ferrari
TOTAL RACES	52 (51 starts)
WINS	24
PODIUM FINISHES	35
POLE POSITIONS	29
FIRST WIN	1950 Monaco Grand Prix
LAST WIN	1957 German Grand Prix
LAST RACE	1958 French Grand Prix

Fangio's feats during 1949 earned him a spot on the Alfa Romeo team, which was hotly tipped for the 1950 World Championship. The Alfa 159 was the fastest and most reliable car on the grid in the early days of Formula 1 and the team duly dominated the first season. Fangio was ultimately beaten to the title by teammate "Nino" Farina in a dramatic final race showdown – he got his revenge by taking the Italian's title the following year.

Having decided to join Maserati for the 1952 season, Fangio suffered serious injuries, including a broken neck, at the Italian Grand Prix. Many thought he would never race again but amazingly he returned the following season. While his Maserati was competitive, it lacked the sheer power of the dominant Ferrari Tipo 500, and he could only finish second in the Championship.

He was back to winning ways in 1954, taking the first of four consecutive World Championship titles, despite switching from Maserati to Mercedes midway through the season. After winning further titles with Mercedes and Ferrari, Fangio would eventually return to Maserati in 1957 to claim his final World Championship at the age of 46. His success with the Italian team was particularly remarkable, given that his car failed at the decisive final race of the 1956 season in Italy. Teammate Peter Collins handed his car over to Fangio part way through the race. The Argentine duly finished second, guaranteeing a fourth Championship.

Fangio retired in 1958, exiting the stage with 24 wins in 51 races, a win ratio of 46.1 per cent – still the highest in the history of Formula 1. Following his death in 1995, former track rival Sir Stirling Moss described him as a "great artist of driving". To some, he remains the greatest Formula 1 driver of all time.

Fangio was all smiles prior to the German Grand Prix in 1954. He set a new lap record in practice and started in pole and eventually went on to win the race.

MIKE
HAWTHORN

Mike Hawthorn became famous for wearing a bow tie at all times, even during races. He's seen here holding the 1958 Glover Trophy after taking the chequered flag at Goodwood.

Mike Hawthorn lived his short life to the full. The first in a long line of English Formula 1 playboys – as famous for his excesses off the track as his successes on it – Hawthorn cemented his place in the history books by claiming the 1958 World Championship. It would be the final chapter of an eventful career.

Born and raised in Yorkshire, England, Hawthorn fell in love with motor sport as a schoolboy. He became a regular visitor to races at the legendary Brooklands circuit in Surrey, enthused by his father's shared passion for the sport. In 1950 at the age of 21, he entered his first race, the Brighton Hill Climb.

Having excelled at driving two-seater cars, Hawthorn found funding to compete in the 1952 Formula 1 World Championship as a private entrant, driving a Formula 2-spec Cooper-Bristol. He finished fourth in his debut race, the Belgian Grand Prix at Spa-Francorchamps, and followed this by taking third at the British Grand Prix.

These feats were enough for Enzo Ferrari to invite Hawthorn to drive for his team, the most prestigious in Formula 1, for the 1953 season. Hawthorn achieved some good results, most notably a great win over Juan Manuel Fangio at the French Grand Prix, but he could only finish fourth in the World Championship.

A series of difficult years followed, with crashes, the death of his father and constant team changes hampering his progress. In 1955, he was heavily involved in the Le Mans 24-Hour disaster, where a dramatic crash led to the death of driver Pierre Levegh and 83 spectators. Hawthorn had been leading the race at the time, and some believe his decision to brake late triggered the tragic chain of events. While Hawthorn was officially cleared of any fault, the incident cast a long shadow over his career.

Hawthorn drove the Ferrari 246/F1 like a man possessed during the 1958 season, finishing in podium positions in seven of the ten races he contested.

STATISTICS

BORN	10th April 1929
NATIONALITY	British
ACTIVE YEARS	1950–58
TEAMS	Ferrari, Vanwall, Maserati, BRM
TOTAL RACES	47 (45 starts)
WINS	3
PODIUM FINISHES	18
POLE POSITIONS	4
FIRST WIN	1953 French Grand Prix
LAST WIN	1958 French Grand Prix
LAST RACE	1958 Moroccan Grand Prix

Hawthorn's career began to pick up when he returned to Ferrari in 1957, making up a strong team that also included fellow Briton Peter Collins. The two would become firm friends, splitting prize money in a bid to better the exploits of Ferrari's third driver, Italian Luigi Musso. Collins died following a crash at the 1958 French Grand Prix, attempting to overtake Hawthorn, who won the race, on a tricky corner.

Despite few race wins, Hawthorn was a worthy winner of the 1958 World Championship. None of his rivals could match Hawthorn's consistency that year, which was backed by the speed and technical brilliance of his Ferrari. He sealed the Championship with a second-place finish at the season-ending Moroccan Grand Prix.

Hawthorn had little time to savour his win, though. He was deeply affected by the death of his teammate and friend, Peter Collins, and announced his retirement at the end of the season. A few months later, Hawthorn lost his life in a car crash, this time after colliding with a lorry near his home in Surrey. He was just 29 years old.

Despite his success in winning the World Championship, Hawthorn is rarely talked about in the reverent tones reserved for fellow early Formula 1 pioneers such as Juan Manuel Fangio, Alberto Ascari and Sir Stirling Moss. His role in a number of fatal crashes is considered a black mark on his career, while his erratic and reckless driving style didn't endear him to other drivers. The fact that he frequently turned up to Grand Prix hungover or, on rare occasions, drunk, hardly helped. It was for these reasons that he failed to produce consistent results for much of his career, something that frequently infuriated his team owners.

Despite these flaws, Hawthorn was a talented driver. His success ushered in a new era of British dominance that would continue throughout the 1960s.

Towards the end of his career, Hawthorn became increasingly aware of the dangers of Formula 1. It was no surprise when he chose to retire at the end of the 1958 season, despite his young age.

STIRLING MOSS

It says a lot about the driving skills of Stirling Moss that he's still widely considered to be one of Formula 1's greatest ever drivers, despite never winning a World Championship. It says even more about his character and sense of fair play that, when British rival Mike Hawthorn was penalised at the 1958 Portuguese Grand Prix, Moss stood up for him and had the decision overturned. In the end, that gesture cost Moss the World Championship.

That Moss was never less than competitive, even in inferior cars, is testament to his immense driving skills. He also had an uncanny knack of getting the best out of the cars he drove, whether sports cars, touring cars or, most famously, Formula 1 cars. It's no wonder many Formula 1 commentators still believe that he was the best driver never to win the World Championship.

Like many drivers of his era, Moss's first taste of motor sport came in hill climbs. By the age of 20 he'd made his way onto the track, securing a place in HWM's Formula 2 Team. He made his Formula 1 debut in 1951, but raced just once, coming eighth in the season-opening Swiss Grand Prix. His decision to stick with unreliable British cars held him back for the next few seasons. When he did get behind the wheel of an Italian car – a Maserati – he finished third at the 1954 Belgian Grand Prix.

Moss's exploits in Belgium caught the eye of the Mercedes Benz team. The team invited him to partner World Champion Juan Manuel Fangio during the 1955 season. The two struck up a great friendship and partnership, and Mercedes dominated the World Championship. Moss made history by becoming the first Briton to win the British Grand Prix (that year held at Aintree, rather than Silverstone), and he finished third in the World Championship, with teammate Fangio securing his third title.

The decision of Mercedes to withdraw from motor sport in the wake of the 1955 Le Mans disaster saw Moss turn to Maserati in 1956. He again pushed Fangio all the way, winning twice and coming second in the World Championship. Moss was persuaded to join the British Vanwall team in 1957 and resumed his battle with the Argentine, again finishing runner up in the Championship.

(inset): Comfortable driving in all conditions, Stirling Moss was one of the only drivers to consistently challenge Juan Manuel Fangio during the 1950s.

Moss won more races than anyone else in the 1958 season. Agonisingly, because of his sporting gesture at the 1958 Portuguese Grand Prix, he missed out on the World Championship by a single point to Mike Hawthorn. In 1961, towards the tail end of his career, he managed to hold off the challenge of the dominant Ferrari team to win the 1960 Monaco Grand Prix in a Lotus that was technically vastly inferior.

Enzo Ferrari tried in vain to persuade Moss to join his team in 1962, but tragedy struck at a non-championship Formula 1 race at Goodwood in April. Moss crashed and was critically injured, spending a month in a coma. A year later he returned to the track to race again, but withdrew after a lap, announcing his immediate retirement from motor sport. It was a low-key end to an exceptional career.

STATISTICS

BORN	17th September 1929
NATIONALITY	British
ACTIVE YEARS	1951–61
TEAMS	Mercedes Benz, Maserati, Vanwall, Rob Walker Cooper, Lotus, HWM
TOTAL RACES	67 (66 starts)
WINS	16
PODIUM FINISHES	24
POLE POSITIONS	16
FIRST WIN	1955 British Grand Prix
LAST WIN	1961 German Grand Prix
LAST RACE	1961 USA Grand Prix

Despite winning 16 Grand Prix over the course of his career, Stirling Moss was unable to claim the prize he cherished most – the Formula 1 World Championship.

British racing driver Stirling Moss
at the wheel of a Maserati 250F
Formula One car, circa 1954.

TECHNICAL REVOLUTION

The history of Formula 1 is one of constant technical development. Yet in the early years of the sport, manufacturers were surprisingly conservative. Formula 1's first decade was largely dominated by factory-made, top-of-the-range sports cars from famous brands such as Alfa Romeo, Ferrari, Mercedes and Maserati.

Amazingly, one of these internationally renowned manufacturers wasn't responsible for the sport's first true technical revolution. Instead, it was a small British manufacturer called Cooper.

Veteran racing mechanic Charles Cooper was the man who made it all happen. He believed that racing cars would be more powerful and efficient if the engine was placed behind the driver's cockpit, close to the rear axle. Given that the most successful racing cars of the period featured the engine at the front of the vehicle, it was a revolutionary idea.

Cooper tried the concept first with 500cc Formula 3 cars and it was an almost instant success. His "mid engine" cars dominated the field. There were still doubts, though, whether Cooper's concept could be applied to more powerful Formula 1 cars.

Experimental versions of Cooper's mid-engine Formula 1 cars made a few appearances in Grand Prix during the mid 1950s, but it wasn't until 1958 that their potential superiority over front-engine cars was proven. With Stirling Moss behind the wheel, the Cooper T45 won the 1958 Argentinian Grand Prix. It was the start of a period of dominance for Cooper's mid-engine cars, with Jack Brabham winning back-to-back World Championships in the T51 – the most powerful and reliable model yet.

By 1961, all manufacturers had switched to mid-engine designs and never looked back. While Cooper's dominance was short-lived, thanks to more sophisticated designs from leading manufacturers, the car remains one of Formula 1's most iconic and ground-breaking designs. It revolutionised the sport forever, and few cars, even today, can boast that accolade.

At the 1958 Argentinian Grand Prix, Stirling Moss benefitted from the innovative design of the Cooper-Climax, which was the first Formula 1 car to place the engine towards the rear of the vehicle.

The 1959 Cooper T51 was Formula 1's first revolutionary car. Its streamlined shape, pointed nose and mid-engine design paved the way for all Formula 1 cars that followed.

1960s

JACK
BRABHAM

Jack Brabham, here shown at the 1967 Daily Mail Race of Champions, used his engineering background to design, build and race his own Formula 1 cars.

Jack Brabham was a genuine one-off. A talented mechanic as well as a determined driver, he used his technical skills to help manufacture cars that ultimately won him a trio of World Championship titles. More remarkably, he won his third title in a car that he'd designed and funded himself, making him the only driver to win both the Drivers and Constructors Championships in a car bearing his own name.

Born and raised in Sydney, Australia, Brabham studied mechanical engineering before working as an engineer in the Royal Australian Air Force. Following the Second World War, he built his first racing car, a Midget Racer, for a US client called Johnny Schonberg. When he decided to quit, Brabham began racing the car himself on dirt tracks around Sydney and was soon champion of New South Wales.

Having decided his racing ambitions would go no further, he was persuaded to reconsider following a chance meeting with fellow engineer

Ron Tauranac. The two would become friends and business partners, with the latter following Brabham to Europe in 1955. Brabham decided to make the switch after spending several winters racing his Cooper-Bristol in New Zealand, where he found he could hold his own against some of the world's best drivers.

While the 1955 season didn't go well, Brabham was offered the chance to work at the Cooper Car Company between races. Working alongside Charles Cooper, Brabham was integral in developing a series of revolutionary mid-engine cars that would later go on to dominate Formula 1 around the turn of the decade.

While the Cooper was being developed, Brabham's results were mediocre. The company tried a number of different designs before eventually settling on the T51, featuring a Climax-4 engine. With the formula perfected by the beginning on 1959, things began to look up for the focused Australian.

Jack Brabham's 1966 World Championship win was particularly sweet for the Australian because it came in the Brabham-Repco BT19, a car he helped to design and build.

STATISTICS

BORN	2nd April 1926
NATIONALITY	Australian
ACTIVE YEARS	1955–70
TEAMS	Cooper, Rob Walker Racing Team, Brabham
TOTAL RACES	128 (126 starts)
WINS	14
PODIUM FINISHES	31
POLE POSITIONS	13
FIRST WIN	1959 Monaco Grand Prix
LAST WIN	1970 South African Grand Prix
LAST RACE	1970 Mexican Grand Prix

Behind the wheel of the revolutionary mid-engine Cooper T-51, Brabham won the season-opening Monaco Grand Prix. Further success at the British Grand Prix followed, with a string of podium finishes helping him claim the 1959 World Championship.

The development of the mid-engine T51 put other manufacturers in a spin. While they went away and worked on their own mid-engine models, Brabham and his trusty Cooper dominated the 1960 season. After being disqualified in Monaco, he went on to win the next five Grand Prix in Europe, storming to a second World Championship crown.

Rule changes in 1961 badly dented his chances of a third straight title, and he found it almost impossible to keep up with the Ferrari drivers. He decided to concentrate instead on building his own manufacturing business with old friend and colleague Ron Tauranac. After quitting the Cooper team, Brabham launched his own in 1962, vowing to build his own Formula 1 car from scratch. The Brabham BT3 made its debut at the 1962 German Grand Prix. It would be four years before Brabham himself would taste success in one of his own cars, though fellow team driver Dan Gurney did win the French Grand Prix at Rouen in 1964.

With a few tweaks and a new engine, Brabham found himself driving the fastest car on the grid in 1966. He took full advantage, winning his third World Championship as a driver, and his first Constructors Championship as a team owner. The Brabham team would go on to win further honours in the years to come, with Denny Hulme driving to the World Championship title in 1967.

Brabham finally retired from racing in 1970 at the age of 44. He sold most of his stake in the Formula 1 team bearing his name to Ron Tauranac, and returned to his native Australia.

Jack Brabham celebrates winning the 1966 British Grand Prix at Brands Hatch, the second of four consecutive victories that helped him secure a third World Championship.

PHIL HILL

It would be fair to say that Phil Hill is one of the lesser-known legends of Formula 1, despite being one of just two US drivers to win the World Championship – and the only man born in the United States to take the crown.

Hill was an unlikely racing driver in many ways. Despite a lengthy career racing sports cars, super cars and Formula 1 cars, he was famously anxious before racing, stalking the grid while chain-smoking cigarettes. He worried constantly, and early in his career suffered from stomach ulcers. Having seen many fellow drivers killed or injured in crashes, he was petrified of becoming another victim. While many of his rivals were loud, brash characters, off the track, he was quiet and introverted. He certainly never fitted the personality profile of the majority of early Formula 1 drivers.

Despite these personality traits, fellow professionals considered Hill to be a good driver. He was renowned for making very few mistakes, and his tactical acumen was legendary. In fact, his tactical driving proved instrumental in helping teammate Mike Hawthorn win the 1958 World Championship.

Hill's Formula 1 career was fairly undistinguished until he joined Ferrari for the 1961 season. Behind the wheel of the fastest car on the grid, he drove his way to the World Championship title.

Hill began his career racing sports cars. After his parents died he bought a Ferrari and plunged himself into the world of sports car racing. He quickly built up a reputation as one of the United States' most talented young drivers, leading Enzo Ferrari to invite him to race for his team at the Le Mans 24-Hour Race in 1955. Hill was left mentally scarred for life by the disaster that unfolded that day but returned to the famous French race on numerous occasions, clinching three wins in the process.

Hill was stalked by fear throughout his Formula 1 career. Petrified of becoming another Formula 1 fatality, he frequently looked worried and anxious before races.

STATISTICS

Hill's feats in US sports car racing earned him a shot at Formula 1 glory with Ferrari in 1958.

BORN	20th April 1927
NATIONALITY	US
ACTIVE YEARS	1958–64, 1966
TEAMS	Maserati, Ferrari, Cooper, Porsche, Automobil Turismo e Sport, Lotus, Eagle
TOTAL RACES	51 (48 starts)
WINS	3
PODIUM FINISHES	16
POLE POSITIONS	6
FIRST WIN	1960 Italian Grand Prix
LAST WIN	1961 Italian Grand Prix
LAST RACE	1966 Italian Grand Prix

Phil Hill smiles for the camera
during the build-up to the 1961
Dutch Grand Prix, a race in which
he came runner-up to Ferrari
teammate Wolfgang van Trips.

Hill was frustrated in sports cars and had a strong desire
to test his skills in Formula 1. Having been rebuffed by Enzo
Ferrari, he bought himself a Maserati and paid for his own
entry into a Grand Prix. Soon after, two Ferrari drivers, Peter
Collins and Luigi Mussi, were killed in quick succession.
Enzo Ferrari turned to Hill and he began to make his mark
in 1959 with a brace of second-placed finishes.

In 1960, he grabbed his first win at the Italian Grand Prix
at Monza, much to the delight of a passionate, Ferrari-mad
home crowd. He followed it up with a another two wins on
his way to the World Championship title the following year,
at Spa-Francorchamps in Belgium and again at Monza.
The latter was tinged with sadness. He barely celebrated
clinching the title, following the tragic death of teammate
Wolfgang von Trips during the race. The media reported that
Hill broke down in tears when he heard the news, though he
later claimed this was not true. "When you've lived as close
to death and danger as long as I have, then your emotional
defences are almost equal to anything," he said.

Perhaps von Tripp's death affected him more than he let on,
because he struggled to rekindle his form in 1962. He left
Ferrari at the end of the year, switching to the ATS team
and later Cooper. He struggled on the track, but continued
to enjoy success in endurance racing.

There was something a little comical about Hill's eventual
retirement. At the end of 1967, he forgot to renew his
international competition licence, thus retiring by accident.
He turned his back on top-line racing for good, occasionally
appearing in historic re-enactments while running a classic
car restoration business close to his home in California.

GRAHAM HILL

Allegedly blessed with less natural ability than many of his major rivals, Graham Hill had to work hard at his driving. The endless hours of practice paid off, with the British driver claiming World Championship titles in 1962 and 1968.

With his swept-back hair, dry humour and trademark pencil moustache, Graham Hill was the epitome of the English gentleman racer. Shorn of the natural racing talents of some of his rivals, through hard work and sheer determination he became one of the most consistent drivers on the Formula 1 scene during the 1960s, and one of the sport's most well-loved personalities.

Along the way, Hill won two World Championship titles, secured a trio of famous wins at the glamorous Monaco Grand Prix, and almost single-handedly revived the fortunes of the ailing Lotus team. By the time he retired in 1975, he'd become the first driver to win the "triple crown" of motor sport – the Le Mans 24-Hour Race, the Indianapolis 500 and the Formula 1 World Championship.

Unlike many of his contemporaries, Hill wasn't a naturally gifted driver. It took him to the age of 24 to pass his driving test, and his skills behind the wheel were initially rough and ready to say the least. Nevertheless, after attending a racing school at Brands Hatch he set his sights on becoming a Formula 1 driver, and worked exceptionally hard, often without pay, to earn opportunities to drive.

Hill's first involvement with professional racing came as a mechanic. He met Lotus team owner Colin Chapman and helped build their 1956 Formula 2 car. When Lotus decided to enter Formula 1 in 1958, Hill persuaded Chapman to give him a spot on the team. He made his driving debut at the 1958 Monaco Grand Prix, keeping pace with the leaders before being forced to retire when one of his wheels came off.

Hill continued to drive for Lotus without success until the end of the 1959. Chapman's Lotuses were unreliable and Hill knew he'd need a better car to satisfy his hunger for Grand Prix wins.

Hill suffered some frustrating years with BRM following his 1962 World Championship win. His 1966 season was blighted by technical problems, leading to a string of forced retirements during races.

STATISTICS

BORN	15th February 1929
NATIONALITY	British
ACTIVE YEARS	1958–75
TEAMS	Lotus, BRM, Brabham, Hill
TOTAL RACES	179 (176 starts)
WINS	14
PODIUM FINISHES	36
POLE POSITIONS	13
FIRST WIN	1962 Dutch Grand Prix
LAST WIN	1969 Monaco Grand Prix
LAST RACE	1975 Monaco Grand Prix

Hill's move to BRM wasn't much of a success to begin with. Following forgettable seasons in 1960 and 1961, he began the 1962 season equipped with a fast, reliable BRM, complete with a V8 engine. Hill was a model of reliability all season, winning the German, Italian and Dutch Grand Prix. He went into the final race of the season, in South Africa, battling it out with British rival Jim Clark for the Championship. Luck was smiling on Hill: Clark's Lotus broke down and Hill took both the race and the title.

For the following three seasons Hill was the man to beat but on each occasion he ended up runner up in the World Championship. In 1966 he won the Indianapolis 500 ahead of British rival Jackie Stewart – a man whose natural talent and smooth driving style Hill envied – and in 1967, was tempted back to Lotus to partner former rival Jim Clark.

As so often happened in the early days of Formula 1, tragedy struck. On the eve of the Spanish Grand Prix, Jim Clark was killed while driving in a Formula 2 race. Lotus boss Colin Chapman was consumed by grief and failed to turn up in Spain. In his absence, Hill took control of the team and won the race, setting himself on course for a second World Championship. As he had done in 1962, he secured the title at the final race of the season.

Hill continued racing with diminishing returns until finally calling it a day in 1975. Just a few months after he retired, the plane he was piloting crashed in heavy fog, killing everyone on board. It was a tragic end to a remarkable career. However, his legacy would live on through his son Damon, who emulated his famous father's feats by becoming the 1996 Formula 1 World Champion.

Hill's win at Germany's Nürburgring in 1962 was only his second Grand Prix victory. He would taste victory a further 12 times before retiring in 1974.

TEAM LOTUS: PIONEERS

In 1958, Lotus Engineering owner Colin Chapman decided the time was right to turn his attention to Formula 1. While his firm had been making sports cars since 1952, and entering them in Formula 2 races since 1957, moving up to motor sport's most prestigious competition was a risky move. Ultimately, it was one that paid off because over the next two decades Lotus became one of the sport's leading teams, earning their success through a combination of technical and commercial transformations.

Things didn't go particularly smoothly on the track to begin with, but thanks to a number of technical innovations, Lotus cars dominated the 1963 season, earning the team the first of seven Constructors World Championships.

The Lotus 25 car used that season was revolutionary: it was the first Formula 1 car to feature a monocoque chassis. Before that, manufacturers had used a "ladder chassis" system, where the body of the vehicle was built separately from the chassis and fitted together. Chapman's monocoque design built the chassis into the body of the car. Combined with careful study of aerodynamics, slowly but surely the Lotus's innovative design became the norm in Formula 1.

Chapman's unique cars, designed following rigorous research and testing, were undoubtedly the most revolutionary and successful during the 1960s and 1970s, even if they did have a tendency to break down (the team's safety record was notoriously poor, with a number of drivers suffering fatal or life-threatening injuries). Lotus drivers won seven World Championships during the 1960s and 1970s, a remarkable record given the company's background.

Chapman's other great innovation was commercial sponsorship. In 1968, Lotus became the first team to carry sponsors' logos on the side of their cars. It was a roaring success and soon, every other team followed suit.

To many observers, the 1967 Lotus 49 remains one of Formula 1's most innovative cars. Many of its innovations, including the monocoque chassis and aerodynamic design, would later become synonymous with Formula 1 cars.

Lotus founder Colin Chapman was one of Formula 1's great innovators but his technically advanced cars were often fragile, unreliable and dangerous to drive.

JOHN
SURTEES

J ohn Surtees was a remarkable competitor. To this day, he's the only man to have won World Championships on two and four wheels, a great testament to his immense skill and versatility. By the time he arrived in Formula 1, he'd already won a staggering seven motorcycling World Championships, winning 38 of the 49 races he competed in across two engine categories (350cc and 500cc). Despite this success, rising through the ranks of Formula 1 to become 1964 World Champion was an astonishing achievement.

The son of a South London motorcycle dealer, Surtees wanted to race motorcycles from an early age. He made his competitive debut aged just 15 and won his first 500cc motorcycle World Championship in 1956 at just 22 years old. He went on to dominate top-level motorbike racing over the next four years, adding a trio of consecutive Isle of Man TT victories to his bulging list of achievements.

Surtees was dabbling with racing cars during his motorcycle-racing career. In 1959, he entered his first race at Goodwood behind the wheel of a Formula 3 Cooper. He enjoyed the experience and decided to make the switch to cars full time – a bold move given the competitive nature of Formula 1. Colin Chapman gave Surtees a chance to race one of his Lotus cars in four races during the 1960 season, and the Londoner duly impressed. He finished second at the British Grand Prix, alerting rival teams to his obvious talents.

Surtees quickly became a man in demand, and frequently moved between teams during the early part of his career. Following some unproductive spells with Cooper and Lola, he transferred to Ferrari in 1963, claiming his first Grand Prix victory at the Nürburgring in Germany. Further podium finishes followed, but a poor end to the season cost him a shot at the World Championship.

STATISTICS

BORN	11th February 1934
NATIONALITY	British
ACTIVE YEARS	1960–72
TEAMS	Lotus, Cooper, Lola, Ferrari, Honda, BRM, McLaren, Surtees
TOTAL RACES	113 (111 starts)
WINS	6
PODIUM FINISHES	24
POLE POSITIONS	8
FIRST WIN	1963 German Grand Prix
LAST WIN	1967 Italian Grand Prix
LAST RACE	1972 Italian Grand Prix

Surtees was a natural racer, able to win races on both two wheels and four. He remains the only man to win World Championships in motorcycling and Formula 1.

John Surtees led from the start of the 1963 German Grand Prix and kept his head to record his first ever Grand Prix win.

John Surtees remains a popular figure in Formula 1 circles, and still makes appearances at motor sport events despite his advancing years.

Things would be so different in 1964. While Surtees endured a poor start to the season, another win in Germany put him back on track. A win at Monza in Italy and two other podium finishes enhanced his Championship credentials, though Surtees would go into the final race of the season trailing leader Graham Hill by a daunting five points. To spice things up further, the great Jim Clark was just four points behind Surtees and could snatch the Championship with a victory.

The scene was set for a classic final Grand Prix of the season in Mexico. Surtees' chances were boosted when Graham Hill crashed out early on, under pressure from the Briton's Ferrari teammate Lorezo Bandini. Jim Clark took the lead, with Surtees trailing in third. When Clark's engine blew up on the final lap, Surtees was able to claim second place and with it, the 1964 World Championship title. It was a dramatic and thrilling conclusion to a topsy-turvy season.

Surtees would never again taste such sweet success. He suffered life-threatening injuries during testing in Canada at the tail-end of 1965, but brilliantly battled back to win the second race of the 1966 season, the Belgian Grand Prix at Spa-Francorchamps. Later in the season he fell out with Ferrari after an argument over his partner at the Le Mans 24-Hour race, and finished the year driving for Cooper.

It was the first of a number of disastrous moves. After brief spells with Honda, BRM and McLaren, Surtees decided to form his own team in 1970. He continued driving with little success until 1972, before retiring to concentrate on running the team. The manufacturer's fortunes didn't improve, and the team folded in 1978. It was an unsatisfying end to Surtees' glittering motor sport career.

JIM
CLARK

Many Formula 1 experts believe that Jim Clark was one of the most naturally gifted drivers ever to grace the track. His record of 25 wins in 72 starts is comparable with other greats of the sport.

In these days of racing driver training programmes, performance pathways and sponsorship-led recruitment, it's unlikely a farmer's son from Scotland would rise through the ranks to become one of the best drivers the world has ever seen.

This is what Jim Clark achieved during the 1960s. Blessed with a gift for racing cars, Clark was famed for being able to get the most out of any car he drove. As the number one driver with Colin Chapman's Lotus team, he was often provided with cars that were innovative, revolutionary, fast and, more often than not, unreliable. For the best part of a decade he tamed the Lotus, getting the best out of their powerful cars. Along the way, Clark won two World Championship titles, and was within a whisker of winning many more.

That Clark is still widely regarded as one of Formula 1's greatest drivers is testament to his immense abilities. Shy and quiet off the track, Clark became an artist when put behind the wheel of a Lotus. "He was so smooth, he was so clean, he drove with such finesse," said fellow World Champion Jackie Stewart. "He never bullied a racing car, he sort of caressed it into doing the things he wanted it to do."

Clark began his ascent to Formula 1 greatness in the 1950s, winning road rallies, hill climbs and track races in a wide range of cars. This versatility would become his trademark, and also earned him a chance with Lotus in the Formula Junior competition. He won his first race for the team in March 1960, finishing ahead of another future Formula 1 World Champion, John Surtees. A few months later, Clark made his Formula 1 debut at the 1960 Dutch Grand Prix, ironically replacing Surtees who had taken time off to race the Isle of Man TT.

Clark struggled at times during the 1967 season thanks to the unreliability of his Lotus 49. He was forced to retire in this race, the German Grand Prix at the Nürburgring.

STATISTICS

BORN	4th March 1936
NATIONALITY	British
ACTIVE YEARS	1960–68
TEAMS	Lotus
TOTAL RACES	73 (72 starts)
WINS	25
PODIUM FINISHES	32
POLE POSITIONS	33
FIRST WIN	1962 Belgian Grand Prix
LAST WIN	1968 South African Grand Prix
LAST RACE	1968 South African Grand Prix

Clark's 1961 season was marred by his involvement with the tragic death of Wolfgang van Trips at the Italian Grand Prix at Monza. When Clark and von Trips' cars collided, the latter was thrown from his Ferrari, suffering fatal injuries. His car careered into a group of spectators lining the course, causing a further 14 deaths. Clark was lucky to escape unharmed.

The following season saw Clark, behind the wheel of the first Formula 1 car to boast a monocoque chassis, just miss out on the World Championship. He was leading the decisive Italian Grand Prix when he was forced to retire with an oil leak, handing the 1962 title to rival Graham Hill.

The disappointment seemed to spur on Clark as he ran away with the World Championship in 1963. He won seven of the ten races, and failed to make it onto the podium only once. More amazingly, he led for more than 73 per cent of the laps he drove that season, a record yet to be matched by any other Formula 1 driver.

Clark was unable to defend his title in 1964, but picked up another six wins in 1965 on the way to a second World Championship. In the same year, he also became the first Formula 1 driver to win the US's most prestigious race, the Indianapolis 500.

After a disappointing year in 1966, Clark was again in the thick of the action in 1967, finishing second in the World Championship behind Denny Hulme. It would be his last hurrah. In 1968, he was tragically killed at a Formula 2 race in Germany. Once again, his unpredictable Lotus had developed a fault.

The world of Formula 1 was shocked and devastated by Clark's death. Fellow driver Chris Amon summed up the mood of the paddock when he said: "If it could happen to Jimmy, what hope do the rest of us have?"

Clark was a likable figure who was popular with fans and rivals alike. His death in 1968 cast a long shadow over the sport.

DENNY HULME

P opularly known as "the bear", straight-talking New Zealander Denny Hulme was a model of consistency on the track. Although he often struggled to match the raw speed of his rivals, he had a knack of picking up good results and rarely finished outside of the top ten.

This consistency came to the fore in 1967, when he picked up two wins and six other top-three finishes to claim his first and only World Championship crown. In the process, he edged out the late, great Jim Clark, securing the title with a third-place finish in Mexico.

It was just reward for a career that took some time to get going. He learnt to drive a truck aged six in his native New Zealand, and began competing in Hill Climbs as a 20-year-old. A move to track racing followed, and in 1959, he jointly won a "driver to Europe" competition. His prize was a scholarship to further his racing career in the UK.

After seeing his friend and fellow scholarship recipient Bruce Lawton killed in a crash during a Formula 2 race, Hulme joined Jack Brabham's racing team as a mechanic. He grew close to Brabham, who tried him out as a driver, first in Formula Junior and later, Formula 2. Hulme's success was enough to earn him a spot in Brabham's Formula 1 team from 1965 onwards.

After winning the World Championship in 1967, Hulme left Brabham to join fellow New Zealander Bruce McLaren's new team. Things went well in the team's first season, with Hulme finishing runner-up to a resurgent Graham Hill in the World Championship. Hulme would be an ever-present for McLaren until 1974, when the on-track death of close friend Peter Revson prompted his retirement.

Hulme continued racing occasionally as an amateur until 1992, when he suffered a heart attack and died while driving in a touring car race.

Denny Hulme may have lacked the speed of his rivals but he more than made up for it with the consistency of his results.

STATISTICS

BORN	18th June 1936
NATIONALITY	New Zealander
ACTIVE YEARS	1965–74
TEAMS	Brabham, McLaren
TOTAL RACES	112
WINS	8
PODIUM FINISHES	33
POLE POSITIONS	1
FIRST WIN	1967 Monaco Grand Prix
LAST WIN	1974 Argentine Grand Prix
LAST RACE	1974 United States Grand Prix

Hulme was calmness personified during his World Championship winning season in 1967. Here he waits on the grid before the French Grand Prix, a race won by his teammate and friend Jack Brabham.

The relationship between Hulme (centre) and Jack Brabham was integral to the success of the latter's team throughout the mid 1960s.

1970s

JOCHEN RINDT

Jochen Rindt was notorious for crashing his cars. This picture was taken at the 1968 Monaco Grand Prix – one of many races he failed to finish.

With his wild, aggressive driving style and passion for speed, Jochen Rindt was a serious accident waiting to happen. One of Formula 1's bad boys, Rindt had risen through the ranks of motor sport in spite of his reckless nature. While he was always exciting to watch, his frequent crashes and "seat of the pants" style would ultimately lead to his downfall.

In the end, there was an air of inevitability about his death during practice for the 1970 Italian Grand Prix at Monza. In a bid to match the speed of his rivals, Rindt had chosen to remove the wings from his Lotus 72 to reduce drag. This was a decision that would prove catastrophic. Under braking, Rindt lost control coming into the Parabolica and careered into the track-side barriers. He was leading the World Championship at the time. A few weeks later, he was confirmed as Formula 1's first (and, to date, only) posthumous World Champion.

Rindt was renowned for a "devil-may-care" attitude and seemed to have a strange sense of his own destiny. "Maybe I will not live to the age of 40," he once told reporters, "but until that time I will have experienced more things in life than anybody else."

Born to a wealthy family in Mainz, Germany, Rindt lost both parents during a Second World War bombing raid, and was subsequently adopted and raised in Austria by his maternal grandparents. He was something of a tear-away teenager, and regularly fell foul of the police for speeding. His passion for fast cars drew him towards racing, first in hill climbs and later touring cars, single-seater sports cars and Formula 2. He became one of the most successful drivers in Formula 2 during the early 1960s, famously beating a trio of future Formula 1 World Champions – Graham Hill, Jim Clark and Denny Hulme – in his second ever Formula 2 race.

STATISTICS

BORN	18th April 1942
NATIONALITY	Austrian
ACTIVE YEARS	1964–70
TEAMS	Alfa Romeo, Ferrari
TOTAL RACES	62 (60 starts)
WINS	6
PODIUM FINISHES	13
POLE POSITIONS	10
FIRST WIN	1964 Austrian Grand Prix
LAST WIN	1970 German Grand Prix
LAST RACE	1970 Italian Grand Prix

Rindt's exciting, occasionally reckless, driving style made him one of the most popular drivers on the circuit.

Rindt got his first taste of Formula 1 with Brabham at the 1964 Austrian Grand Prix. He subsequently joined Cooper for the 1965 season, impressing rivals by finishing third in the 1966 World Championship in what was widely regarded as an uncompetitive car. A series of disappointing seasons with Cooper and Brabham followed, before he joined Colin Chapman's Lotus team for the 1969 season.

While his relationship with Chapman was strained from the start, it did prove fruitful. Rindt won his first Formula 1 race: the United States Grand Prix at Watkins Glen in 1969. It would be another 12 months before he would be behind the wheel of a car befitting his talents.

Chapman eventually delivered Rindt a car that matched his aspirations: the Lotus 72. Going into the 1970 season, much was expected of the car but Chapman was still tinkering with the design. Rindt was furious that he had to enter the Monaco Grand Prix in the outdated Lotus 49 but nevertheless scored a remarkable victory. After making his way through the field, he set a string of fastest laps to reel in leader Jack Brabham, passing him on the final corner.

Once the Lotus 72 finally arrived, Rindt was unstoppable. He won consecutive Grand Prix in the Netherlands, France, Britain and Germany to lead the World Championship for the first time in his career. Saddened by the deaths of friends Bruce McLaren and Piers Courage in recent races, he told his wife he would retire if he won the World Championship.

Sadly, fate intervened. Rindt's death at the Italian Grand Prix on 5th September 1970, rocked Formula 1. The sport was still mourning Rindt's loss at the season-ending United States Grand Prix, where Emerson Fittipaldi's win for Lotus confirmed the Austrian driver's World Championship win.

Sitting in his Lotus before free practice at the 1970 Italian Grand Prix, Rindt looked apprehensive. Perhaps he had an uneasy sense of his own destiny because he was killed in a crash later that afternoon.

SAFETY FIRST

The death of Jochen Rindt at Monza in September 1970 was neither the first, nor would it be the last, tragedy for Formula 1. Serious injury and death have stalked Formula 1 since its formative years, with ten drivers losing their lives in the sport's first decade alone. Rindt was the 27th Formula 1 driver to lose his life at a Grand Prix since 1950.

At the time of Rindt's death, safety was a hot topic. The Grand Prix Drivers Association – the drivers' group founded in 1961 to campaign for greater safety measures – had already forced the FIA to move the 1970 German Grand Prix from the Nürburgring following concerns about the dangerous nature of the infamously high-speed track. The death of German driver Gerhard Mitter in 1969 was the fifth fatality at the track dubbed "the Green Hell".

This was not the first time the Grand Prix Drivers Association had forced the FIA to act. Between 1963 and 1965 its lobbying resulted in improvements to fuel tank construction, the widening of cockpits to allow easier escape following crashes, and the introduction of mandatory fireproof overalls and unbreakable helmets. The Spa Francorchamps track in Belgium, another high-speed circuit famed for its dangerous nature, was also redesigned following a 1969 boycott by the Grand Prix Drivers Association.

Rindt's death wasn't as much a wake-up call as a reminder of how far Formula 1 still had to go before it could be considered "safe". The Grand Prix Drivers Association, spurred on by tireless safety campaigner Jackie Stewart, continued to pile on the pressure. Eventually, their demands were met, but it was only in the 1980s that the death count began to drop. Shockingly, following Rindt's accident there were nine more fatalities during the 1970s. Today, deaths are rare (the most recent were Ayrton Senna and Roland Ratzenberger in 1994) but Formula 1 remains a dangerous pursuit for its protagonists.

James Hunt was lucky to escape after a number of his crashes, including this altercation with John Watson's Brabham at the 1977 United States Grand Prix West.

High-speed crashes and pile-ups have long been a feature in Formula 1, but it was only in the 1970s that the sport finally took steps to address their often-tragic consequences.

JACKIE
STEWART

Most modern motor sport fans tend to think of Jackie Stewart as an elder statesman of Formula 1. A popular personality, clad in trademark tartan hat, Stewart's tireless work behind the scenes has helped guarantee Grand Prix racing in Great Britain for the immediate future.

Stewart remains one of the greatest drivers of his generation. Blessed with natural talent and the ability to get great results in inferior cars, the popular Scot won three World Championships over the course of a nine-year career. His tally of 27 wins makes him the second most successful British driver in Formula 1 history, after Nigel Mansell.

Off the track, Stewart campaigned tirelessly for greater safety measures. He was also commercially astute, successfully arguing for higher salaries for Grand Prix drivers at a time when the sport's popularity was rising rapidly. He believed that drivers were putting themselves at huge risk every time they took to the track, and as a result their salaries should reflect this element of danger. In this regard, he was a trendsetter.

Stewart's first love was shooting, but when he failed to qualify for the Great Britain team for the 1960 Olympics, he decided to follow his brother Jimmy's lead and try motor sport instead. He rapidly rose through the ranks, gaining great success for Ken Tyrrell's team in Formula 3 before signing a Formula 1 contract with BRM in 1965.

Stewart hit the ground running during his debut season in Formula 1, tasting victory for the first time at the 1965 Italian Grand Prix. Remarkably, he showed a mastery of the sport that other more experienced drivers failed to match, and came third in the World Championship behind fellow Britons Jim Clark and Graham Hill.

Jackie Stewart's record of 27 Grand Prix victories has been surpassed only by one British driver, 1992 Champion Nigel Mansell.

STATISTICS

BORN	11th June 1939
NATIONALITY	British
ACTIVE YEARS	1965–73
TEAMS	BRM, Matra, March, Tyrrell
TOTAL RACES	100 (99 starts)
WINS	27
PODIUM FINISHES	43
POLE POSITIONS	17
FIRST WIN	1965 Italian Grand Prix
LAST WIN	1973 German Grand Prix
LAST RACE	1973 United States Grand Prix (did not start)

During the 1970 season, Jackie Stewart struggled in Ken Tyrrell's March-Ford car. In this race, the 1970 Monaco Grand Prix, Stewart was forced to retire with technical troubles.

Stewart was proud of
his Scottish roots and
his tartan-flecked racing
helmet and hats became a
trademark on and off
the track.

Following a couple of unsuccessful seasons, Stewart once again joined forces with Ken Tyrrell, the man who'd given him his break in Formula racing, at the Matra Team in 1968. It was an inspired move. He won his first race for two years in the Netherlands and scored a famous victory in torrential rain at the Nürburgring. Stewart later described it as a "teeth gritting effort", as he drove almost blind due to the appallingly heavy rain. He finished the season with three wins and headed into 1969 as the man to beat.

Stewart was in scorching form that season. He won the first two races of the season in South Africa and Spain, before being forced to retire with car troubles in Monaco. It was a minor setback and he won four of the next five races to take an almost unassailable lead in the World Championship. A fourth-place finish in Mexico confirmed his first World Championship title.

After a disappointing 1970 season, Stewart was back to his mercurial best in 1971. Driving a V8 Tyrrell, he frequently got the better of higher-powered and much-fancied cars, including the lauded V12 Ferrari. He became famous for going out hard from the start, establishing a lead and controlling the race. They were tactics that earned Stewart six more wins and a second World Championship title.

Stewart scored his final World Championship win in 1973, again for Tyrrell. Having already won five races by the time he got to the United States Grand Prix, he'd already secured the title. Stewart had vowed to retire after this race – his 100th – but never even started. Tyrrell withdrew his entry following the death of teammate Francois Cevert in qualifying. It was a low key end to Stewart's brilliant Formula 1 career.

EMERSON FITTIPALDI

With a brother who was also a driver and a father who was one of Brazil's leading motor sport journalists, it is unsurprising that Emerson Fittipaldi was drawn to racing. Even so, few expected the boy from Brazil to be an instant success in Formula 1, becoming one of sport's youngest ever champions when he secured the 1972 World Championship, aged 25 years and 273 days.

In the years that followed, Fittipaldi showed his class, finishing runner-up twice and adding another World Championship title in 1974. Arguably, he had the talent to add more World Championships, but in 1976 he made the decision to set up his own Formula 1 team with his brother Wilson. It was a move that cost him dearly: he added only two podium finishes in five years and quit Formula 1 in 1980, a shadow of his former self.

By the time he arrived in Formula 1 in 1970, Fittipaldi had already demonstrated his driving skill. He drove with a combination of control and instinct, a trait that would become synonymous with great Formula 1 champions.

Fittipaldi's entry into Formula 1 came via Formula 3, and before that, Formula Vee and Formula Ford. He was Brazilian champion in both Karting and Formula Vee before deciding to move to England in 1969 to pursue his dream of racing in Formula 1. He spoke no English, and worked as a mechanic to fund the purchase of his own Formula Ford car.

Halfway through the 1969 season, he made the step up to Formula 3. Remarkably, he scored enough points to win the Championship. With such impressive early success, it was unsurprising that Fittipaldi caught the attention of Lotus boss Colin Chapman, who gave him his Formula 1 debut at the 1970 British Grand Prix. Following the death of Jochen Rindt at the Italian Grand Prix, Fittipaldi started at the United States Grand Prix. He produced a stunning drive to secure his first Formula 1 win, in only his fourth start.

Despite driving the revolutionary Lotus 72 in 1971, Fittipaldi struggled to repeat this early success. It was a different story in 1972, though, when he won five of the 12 races, following it up with six consecutive podium finishes to clinch his first World Championship crown.

(inset): Fittipaldi sacrificed the opportunity of winning many more World Championships by setting up his own team with his brother. The Fittipaldi car, seen here at the 1976 Monaco Grand Prix, was rarely competitive.

The following season, Fittipaldi was given a run for his money by teammate Ronnie Peterson. Fittipaldi was furious when Peterson won the final Grand Prix of the season, dashing his chances of winning the World Championship. Had the Swede followed team orders, Fittipaldi may have scored enough points to overtake Jackie Stewart in the title race.

Irritated by this perceived disloyalty, Fittipaldi moved to McLaren, a switch that resulted in a second World Championship title in 1974. It was a battle all the way with Niki Lauda and Clay Regazzoni. When the latter struggled in the final race of the season, Fittipaldi pounced, with fourth place being enough to secure the title. Although Fittipaldi finished runner up in the Championship in 1975, he would not taste World Championship success again. Following five disastrous years running his own team, he retired in 1980, ruing what could have been if he had stayed with McLaren.

Fittipaldi celebrates his 1972 British Grand Prix victory, one of five wins in his first World Championship winning season.

STATISTICS

BORN	12th December 1946
NATIONALITY	Brazilian
ACTIVE YEARS	1970–80
TEAMS	Lotus, McLaren, Fittipaldi Automotive
TOTAL RACES	149 (144 starts)
WINS	14
PODIUM FINISHES	35
POLE POSITIONS	6
FIRST WIN	1970 United States Grand Prix
LAST WIN	1975 British Grand Prix
LAST RACE	1980 United States Grand Prix

Emerson Fittipaldi's focus in the 1974 season saw him regain the World Championship that he'd lost so narrowly the previous year.

NIKI LAUDA

Niki Lauda, nicknamed "The Rat" for his prominent front teeth, was rarely happier than when he was celebrating a Grand Prix victory.

Niki Lauda's legendary status within Formula 1 circles was hard earned, to say the least. While he would eventually go on to win a trio of World Championship titles and achieve worldwide fame thanks to his on-track battles with British rival James Hunt, he made plenty of sacrifices along the way.

Lauda paid for his entry into motor sport by taking out massive loans. He teetered on the edge of bankruptcy several times and ended up with severe facial burns following a near-fatal crash at the Nürburgring in 1976. That he came back, reclaimed his title and won his third crown in 1984 by half a point from teammate Alain Prost (the slimmest margin in Formula 1 history) is credit to his tenacity, tireless worth ethic and drive to succeed.

From an early age, Lauda dedicated his life to making it in motor sports. With Formula 1 his aim, he took out loans to fund his way through the lower categories. Results were mixed and Lauda found his path to Formula 1 blocked by more successful drivers. He took the bold – some would say risky – step of taking out a huge loan against his life insurance in order to buy a place on March's 1972 Formula 2 team. Lauda impressed enough to be offered the chance to try his hand in the team's underperforming Formula 1 car.

While it offered Lauda a chance to fulfil his dreams, all did not go to plan. He finished the 1972 season in further debt and secured a contract with BRM only by taking out additional loans. Through sheer hard work, better results started to come and BRM offered to extend his contract into 1974. However, when teammate Clay Regazzoni moved to Ferrari, Regazzoni persuaded Enzo Ferrari to offer Lauda a chance, too. As part of the deal, the legendary team principal paid off Lauda's debts.

Lauda pushed his Ferrari 312T during practice for the 1976 German Grand Prix. His race ended in near tragedy when the car caught fire following a heavy crash. Only the quick thinking of his fellow drivers saved him.

STATISTICS

BORN	22nd ≠≠≠ February 1949
NATIONALITY	Austrian
ACTIVE YEARS	1971–79, 1982–85
TEAMS	March, BRM, Ferrari, Brabham, McLaren
TOTAL RACES	177 (171 starts)
WINS	25
PODIUM FINISHES	54
POLE POSITIONS	24
FIRST WIN	1974 Spanish Grand Prix
LAST WIN	1985 Dutch Grand Prix
LAST RACE	1985 Australian Grand Prix

It was a decision that would soon pay dividends for Ferrari. After a promising 1974 where he was in contention for the title in one of the team's less-impressive cars, Lauda dominated the 1975 season. He won five times to secure his first World Championship and Ferrari's first since 1964.

The 1976 season would go down in folklore for many reasons. Lauda hit the top of the drivers standings early on and by the time the German Grand Prix came around, he had built up an almost unassailable 30-plus point lead over James Hunt. Disaster struck at the Nürburgring, when Lauda's Ferrari spun off the track, hit a bank and burst into flames. He was pulled from the wreckage by four fellow drivers but suffered several broken bones and severe burns. He was rushed to hospital and read the last rites by a priest.

Amazingly, he survived, and six weeks later was behind the wheel of the Ferrari, determined to stop Hunt, who had cut his Championship lead in his absence to three points. What followed at the final race of the season in Japan has become the stuff of legend. In appalling weather conditions, Mario Andretti won the race, Lauda gave up because of the hazardous conditions and Hunt eventually finished third to win the World Championship.

Lauda, now sporting permanent facial scars following his crash in Germany, won his second World Championship in 1977 and promptly parted company with Ferrari. A couple of disappointing seasons with Brabham followed, before he made the surprise decision to retire in 1979 to concentrate on founding his own airline.

Lauda returned to Formula 1 in 1982, primarily to earn money to put back into Lauda Air, signing with McLaren. He won a remarkable third and final World Championship title in 1984 before calling it a day for good in 1985.

Lauda showed huge guts and determination to return to racing following his near fatal crash, the scars of which could be seen on his face for years to come.

HUNT vs LAUDA

Given the storyline of the 1976 Formula 1 season, it is unsurprising that the rivalry between James Hunt and Niki Lauda would end up being made into a Hollywood film. That 2013's *Rush* is largely faithful to real-life events is testament to just how remarkable the "Hunt-Lauda season" really was.

While very different people – Lauda hardworking and intense, Hunt talented but impulsive – the two drivers were actually good friends off the track. Of course, it is the on-track tussles that everyone remembers, and in 1976 they came thick and fast.

In the early rounds of the Championship, Hunt would often take pole, only to be denied victory by Lauda. Although Hunt bounced back with multiple victories of his own, he was disqualified at the British Grand Prix in July. The race was awarded to Lauda, who held a healthy 35-point lead over Hunt in the Championship.

The following race at the Nürburgring in Germany changed the course of Formula 1 history. While Lauda ended the day fighting for his life in hospital following a horrific crash, Hunt won the Grand Prix to kickstart a comeback that would force the Austrian to return to racing just six weeks later at the Italian Grand Prix. Hunt, now with his tail up, won the next two races to set up a thrilling finale in Japan.

What followed was, even by Formula 1 standards, remarkable. In dreadful, wet conditions, Lauda took the decision to retire after two laps, stating he was struggling to see due to complications with his Nürburgring injuries, which had yet to fully heal. Hunt battled back in the final three laps to grab third place, and the points he needed to pip Lauda to the title by a single point. It was a fittingly dramatic end to Formula 1's most famous season.

Hunt and Lauda enjoyed many tussles on the track, including this famous duel on the final lap of the 1975 Dutch Grand Prix, a race won by the Briton.

Niki Lauda (left) and James Hunt were friends off the track, despite their intense rivalry on it. Here they are pictured following a collision at the 1978 Belgian Grand Prix.

JAMES
HUNT

James Hunt was the epitome of the Formula 1 playboy; a man whose international celebrity owed as much to his notorious womanising and hard-drinking lifestyle as his remarkable feats on the track. Hunt boasted of sleeping with thousands of women – sometimes minutes before races – and would regularly knock back drinks before climbing into his car to start a Grand Prix.

As a driver he was similarly impulsive, as addicted to driving fast as he was to wooing women. This made him hugely popular with fans, though his talent on the track was nowhere near as great as many of his rivals. Nevertheless, he succeeded where many more talented drivers failed, beating rival Niki Lauda to the 1976 World Championship in a final-race shoot-out.

Hunt was born into a wealthy British family and wanted for little growing up. He fell in love with Formula 1 after watching his first race, aged 18. He asked his parents for financial backing to fund his dream of becoming world champion but they refused. Instead, he bought himself a cheap Mini and did it up on a shoestring budget.

During his early years racing Minis and later Formula 3, he earned a reputation as something of a wild child. Fall-outs with rivals and teammates were common and his reckless driving style earned him the nickname "Hunt the Shunt". In truth, few thought he would ever make it to Formula 1 – he was just too impatient.

Fortunately for Hunt, he found a soul mate in Formula 2 team owner Lord Hesketh. The eccentric millionaire had money to burn and a passion for women and champagne. He had no problems funding Hunt's Formula 1 dream and in 1973, decided to switch his team's ambitions from Formula 2 to Formula 1.

It was only after he signed for the Malboro-sponsored McLaren team in 1976, that James Hunt became competitive.

STATISTICS

BORN	29th August 1947
NATIONALITY	British
ACTIVE YEARS	1973–79
TEAMS	Hesketh, McLaren, Wolf
TOTAL RACES	93 (92 starts)
WINS	10
PODIUM FINISHES	23
POLE POSITIONS	14
FIRST WIN	1975 Dutch Grand Prix
LAST WIN	1977 Japanese Grand Prix
LAST RACE	1979 Monaco Grand Prix

Despite his laidback attitude and playboy lifestyle, James Hunt would get notoriously nervous before races, often being sick moments before he got in his car.

By 1978, when this photo was taken, Hunt had lost most of the drive and determination that saw him become 1976 World Champion.

The racing establishment dismissed Hunt and Hesketh as glamour-chasing amateurs and there was arguably a grain of truth in this. Hesketh's interest in racing was conditioned by a love of after-parties and fast cars rather than a deep-rooted love of the sport. However, results were nowhere near as bad as many critics predicted. Hunt finished the 1973 season with a second place finish at the United States Grand Prix and grabbed another three podium finishes in 1974.

It was in the 1975 season where Hunt finally began to look the part. He beat Niki Lauda – a man he would become synonymous with during their epic battle for the title in 1976 – to win the Dutch Grand Prix. A string of podium finishes helped him to finish fourth in the Drivers Championship.

Hesketh finally ran out of money at the end of 1975, leaving Hunt without a drive for 1976. However, Emerson Fittipaldi's decision to quit McLaren – a team very much on the up with a car capable of challenging for honours – opened up an opportunity for the Briton and he grasped it with both hands.

After a turbulent and exciting season full of drama, Hunt and Lauda headed to the final race separated by just three points. In torrential rain, and with the problems of a flooded track to deal with, Lauda retired early, citing problems with his vision. Hunt stuck at it, clawing his way back from fifth on the closing laps to claim third, and with it, his first World Championship crown.

Hunt struggled to regain this form in later years, and after a disastrous opening to the 1979 season decided to call it a day. Instead he headed for the commentary box, where his forthright and outspoken views provided the perfect foil to the excitable Murray Walker on BBC television. Eventually, his party-hard lifestyle caught up with him and he died of a heart attack, aged 45, in 1993.

MARIO
ANDRETTI

Andretti was already a star in US racing when he drove to pole position at the 1968 United States Grand Prix on his first appearance in a Formula 1 car.

Few drivers can claim to be as adaptable as Mario Andretti. Seemingly in love with racing, the Italian-born US driver successfully turned his hand to dirt-track racing, Champ Cars, IndyCars, Formula 1 and long-distance sports car racing, over a career spanning four decades. Andretti remains the only driver in the history of motor sport to have won the Formula 1 World Championship, the IndyCar series, the Daytona 500 and the Indianapolis 500.

Andretti's story is even more remarkable given his formative years in war-torn Italy were spent in a camp for displaced people. Following the Second World War, Andretti was attracted to racing by the feats of Italian Formula 1 hero Alberto Ascari. In 1955, aged 15, his family moved to the United States. Over the next 50 years, Andretti would do his best to follow the American dream.

It was the early 1960s when Andretti first started racing on local dirt tracks with his brother Aldo. Success in sprint and stock car events led to an IndyCar debut in 1964. The following season, Andretti came third on his Indianapolis 500 debut (behind Formula 1 high-flier Jim Clark) and became the youngest ever winner of the USAC National Championship, aged just 25.

Andretti first dabbled in Formula 1 in 1968, driving for Colin Chapman's Lotus team in the United States Grand Prix at Watkins Glen. He made an instant impression, grabbing pole position on his first outing at the track. While he was forced to retire from the race with clutch problems, the naturalised US driver had given Formula 1 fans a taste of his talents. There would be plenty more glimpses of greatness before Andretti would finally commit to Formula 1 full time in 1975, including a memorable first Formula 1 win at the 1971 South African Grand Prix.

Throughout his career, Andretti hopped between Formula 1 and IndyCar. Here he is seen behind the wheel in an IndyCar race in October 1978.

STATISTICS

BORN	28th February 1940
NATIONALITY	US
ACTIVE YEARS	1968–1972, 1974–1982
TEAMS	Lotus, March, Ferrari, Panelli, Alfa Romeo, Williams
TOTAL RACES	129
WINS	12
PODIUM FINISHES	19
POLE POSITIONS	18
FIRST WIN	1971 South African Grand Prix
LAST WIN	1978 Dutch Grand Prix
LAST RACE	1982 Caesar's Palace Grand Prix

As a full-time Formula 1 driver, Andretti failed to find the right team to match his aspirations until reuniting with Colin Chapman's Lotus team in 1977. He won four races in his first full season for the British outfit, with five additional podium finishes leaving him third in the World Championship at the end of the year. He may have done better had the Lotus 78 not been plagued by reliability issues, a constant issue with Colin Chapman's unpredictable cars.

Chapman perfected the car for the start of the 1978 season, and Andretti took full advantage. He was a model of consistency throughout the year, winning six times to take the title. In fact, he failed to finish on the podium in only three of the 16 races that season – form that any World Champion would be proud of. Unfortunately, his moment of glory at Monza – the track where his childhood idol Alberto Ascari had excelled – was overshadowed by the tragic death of teammate Ronnie Peterson.

Andretti continued full-time in Formula 1 with dwindling returns until 1981, when he decided to return to the IndyCar circuit. He did race twice more in Formula 1 the following year as a favour to Ferrari following the death of Gilles Villeneuve, but his time in the sport was up.

It was nowhere near the end of his racing career, though. He won a fourth IndyCar Championship title in 1984 at the age of 44, and continued racing well into his fifties. He claimed his final IndyCar victory in 1993, aged 53, becoming the only man to have won races in four decades.

Today Andretti is rightly considered one of the all-time greats of US racing. He's also head of a racing dynasty. Having watched both his sons follow in his footsteps, he now cheers on grandson Marco in the IndyCar series.

Andretti is pictured here before the 1977 Monaco Grand Prix, a race in which he could finish only fifth.

JODY
SCHEKTER

The 979 Formula 1 World Champion, Jody Schekter, was something of a one-off. Initially regarded as a young, reckless speed freak with the uncanny knack of causing crashes, he reined in his instincts enough to become a threat at the front of the grid. Even so, many were surprised when Schekter joined Ferrari in 1979 and drove away with the World Championship. In the process, he became Formula 1's first – and so far only – South African World Champion.

There was little in Schekter's early racing career to suggest he had the discipline to make it in Formula 1. In his first ever race in motor sport, he was black-flagged for dangerous driving. Schekter went on to earn a reputation for being the most aggressive driver in South Africa. In 1970, victory in the South African Formula Ford Championship earned him a move to Europe, via a driver scholarship programme.

It didn't take long for his reputation as a driver-to-watch to bring him to the attention of the McLaren team. Eighteen months after his arrival in England, he made his Formula 1 debut at the 1972 United States Grand Prix. He looked good for the most part, but almost inevitably crashed out. McLaren sent him down to Formula 2 to hone his skills in 1973 and it wasn't long before he was back in Formula 1. He caused consternation at the 1973 French Grand Prix when he collided with reigning World Champion Emerson Fittipaldi. The Brazilian was furious, telling reporters: "This madman is a menace to himself and everybody else and does not belong in Formula 1." Things didn't improve in his next race at Silverstone, when he spun off and inadvertently caused a huge pile-up.

Schekter began making more of an effort to curb his natural recklessness when he witnessed at close hand the death of French driver Francois Cevert at the 1973 United States Grand Prix. "From then on all I was trying to do in Formula 1 was save my life," Schekter later admitted.

Things started to improve on the track following his move to Tyrrell in 1974. He grabbed his first win at the Swedish Grand Prix – a venue where he would later become the only man to win a race in a six-wheeled car, the Tyrrell P34 – and followed it up with victory at the British Grand Prix. He ended the 1974 season in third place in the World Championship, which was an accurate reflection of his newfound maturity as a driver.

(inset): Scheckter recorded his best result of the 1980 season at the United States Grand Prix West, where he finished fifth.

A move to the Wolf team in 1977 brought him one position closer to the World Championship he craved, but it wasn't until he teamed up with Canadian Gilles Villeneuve at Ferrari in 1979 that things really went to plan. Despite Villeneuve boasting more raw speed – something of a surprise, given Schekter's reckless history – the South African proved to be the more consistent of the two drivers. He won in Belgium, Monaco and Italy, and only failed to score points in three of the 15 Grand Prix contested that season. He was a more than worthy World Champion.

Schekter finished the following season with two solitary points. He promptly retired at the end of the season. Today, Schekter spends his time as an organic farmer in Hampshire, England.

STATISTICS

BORN	29th January 1950
NATIONALITY	South African
ACTIVE YEARS	1972–80
TEAMS	McLaren, Tyrrell, Wolf, Ferrari
TOTAL RACES	113 (112 starts)
WINS	10
PODIUM FINISHES	33
POLE POSITIONS	3
FIRST WIN	1974 Swedish Grand Prix
LAST WIN	1979 Italian Grand Prix
LAST RACE	1980 United States Grand Prix

Jody Scheckter, complete with a distinctive mop of curly hair, infuriated other Formula 1 drivers during his early years in the sport, and was the cause of many crashes.

1980s

ALAN JONES

As the son of an Australian racing legend, many would have expected Alan Jones to have his dreams of Formula 1 success funded by his father. While Stan Jones, winner of the 1959 Australian Drivers Championship, was supportive of Alan's ambitions, he lacked the funds to bankroll him. Instead, Alan was forced to move to Europe and eke out an existence while working his way up the racing ladder.

For the straight-talking Australian, it was not easy. When he moved to Europe in 1967, he barely had enough money to feed himself, let alone pay for his racing dreams. Then, when he did make it into Formula 1, he found himself shunted between teams, driving in uncompetitive cars and seen as little more than a fill-in with potential. Eventually, though, he got his big break, joining Williams for the 1980 season. He ended the year as World Champion, delivering the team's first significant success.

Like many other Formula 1 drivers, Jones' first taste of racing was on the karting circuit as a raw but enthusiastic teenager. He enjoyed some mild success and decided that he wanted to emulate his father by competing in Formula 1. After leaving school, he worked in his father's car dealership and began racing a Mini. With the dealership struggling, Jones decided to travel to England and throw himself into the European motor-sport scene.

Jones spent five years living a hand-to-mouth existence, devoting what time he could searching for a break in racing. By 1973, he found himself at the small GRD team, racing Formula 3 cars. He gained some good results and showed enough promise to catch the attention of wealthy racing enthusiast Harry Stiller. In 1975, Stiller bought an old Hesketh Formula 1 car and Jones made his Formula 1 debut. However, after five races Stiller pulled the plug, leaving Jones without a drive.

STATISTICS

BORN	2nd November 1946
NATIONALITY	Australian
ACTIVE YEARS	1975–1981, 1983, 1985–86
TEAMS	Hesketh, Hill, Surtees, Shadow, Williams, Arrows, Haas Lola
TOTAL RACES	117 (116 starts)
WINS	12
PODIUM FINISHES	24
POLE POSITIONS	6
FIRST WIN	1977 Austrian Grand Prix
LAST WIN	1981 Caesar's Palace Grand Prix
LAST RACE	1986 Australian Grand Prix

During his final season in 1986, Alan Jones found himself behind the wheel of a notoriously unreliable Team Haas car.

Alan Jones was the epitome of a straight-talking Australian, a trait that made him immensely popular with rivals and fans alike.

Thanks to the assistance of technical director Patrick Head (left), Alan Jones' Williams was the most competitive car on the grid during his World Championship winning season in 1980.

Jones thought he had secured another break when the Embassy Hill team drafted him in to replace the injured Rolf Stommelen at the 1975 German Grand Prix. He finished fifth, but was pushed back down to Formula 5000 when Stommelen returned. The collapse of the team at the end of the year following the death of Graham Hill, once again left Jones without a drive.

John Surtees came to his rescue, offering him a place in his team for the 1976 season. Jones competed well, collecting seven World Championship points, but his relationship with Surtees soured. He decided his time in Formula 1 was up, so moved to the United States to race on the USAC circuit.

Jones was back behind the wheel of a Formula 1 car in 1977, replacing the late Tom Pryce at the Shadow team at short notice. It was a move that would reignite his career. Jones drove brilliantly to win the 1977 Austrian Grand Prix – his first victory in Formula 1 – and was asked by Frank Williams to join his new team for the 1978 season.

Finally, Jones was in the right place at the right time. The Williams team had a decent car and plenty of financial backing. Jones showed the potential of the FW07 car by winning four races in 1979, enabling him to finish third in the World Championship.

Then, in 1980, Jones enjoyed the season he'd been dreaming about since he was a small boy. He won five races and secured another five podium finishes to claim his first World Championship title.

Due to a combination of an unreliable car and a bitter relationship with teammate Carlos Reutemann, Jones couldn't repeat the feat in 1981. He promptly retired, only to make occasional unwise returns to the track for uncompetitive teams in coming years. He finally called it a day for good in 1986.

NELSON PIQUET

Like Ayrton Senna in later years, Nelson Piquet was a superstar in motorsport-mad Brazil. Here he concentrates on the task in hand prior to the 1989 Brazilian Grand Prix, during his second season with Lotus.

When behind the wheel of a competitive car, Nelson Piquet was a model of consistency. Unlike other multiple World Champions such as Alain Prost, Michael Schumacher and Sebastian Vettel, Piquet did not dominate during his three Championship winning seasons in 1981, 1983 and 1987, and remarkably he never won more than four races in any one campaign. Yet on each of these occasions, his knack of picking up podium finishes got him across the line.

Piquet was not always popular with fellow drivers, or even the teams he drove for. He would demand that teams were built around him, which put him at loggerheads with teammates, mechanics and officials alike. He was once memorably described by Nigel Mansell as "a vile man", and famously told reporters: "I don't want to make friends with anyone. I don't give a shit for fame. I just want to win."

Piquet's greatest strength was arguably his single-mindedness. He showed this early in life, by turning his back on a promising career in professional tennis – his father's dream – to race karts. He was phenomenally successful, winning back-to-back Brazilian Karting Championships in 1971 and 1972.

Piquet's route into Formula 1 came via lower formulae. After winning the Brazilian Formula Vee Championship in 1976, he moved to Europe in 1977. In 1977, he won the British Formula 3 Championship. The same year, he made his first tentative steps into Formula 1, racing privately entered Ensign and McLaren cars. It was enough to earn him a place in Bernie Ecclestone's Brabham team for the 1979 season.

Brabham struggled with reliability issues all year, with the team's two cars finishing just six races between them. At the end of the season, teammate Niki Lauda retired and Piquet became the team's lead driver for the 1980 season.

Nelson Piquet recorded 23 wins in total during his long and distinguished career, a feat that makes him the 12th most successful Formula 1 Grand Prix winner to date.

STATISTICS

BORN	17th August 1952
NATIONALITY	Brazilian
ACTIVE YEARS	1978–91
TEAMS	Ensign, private McLaren, Brabham, Williams, Lotus, Benetton
TOTAL RACES	207 (204 starts)
WINS	23
PODIUM FINISHES	60
POLE POSITIONS	24
FIRST WIN	1980 United States Grand Prix West
LAST WIN	1991 Canadian Grand Prix
LAST RACE	1991 Australian Grand Prix

Being "top dog" seemed to inspire Piquet, as he started the 1980 season with a second place finish at the Argentinian Grand Prix. He went on to win three times, putting him top of the World Championship standings with two races to go. However, back-to-back retirements as a result of technical failures allowed Alan Jones to beat Piquet to the title.

Piquet was now more fired up than ever and bounced back impressively in 1981. After winning three times and claiming a string of podium finishes, he went into the final race of the season with a slender lead over perennial runner-up Carlos Reutemann. Piquet suffered badly from heat exhaustion throughout the final race of the season in Las Vegas, but somehow finished fifth to secure his first World Championship.

Following a poor year in 1982, Piquet was back to his best in 1983, and secured a second World Championship. He won two of the final three races of the season to beat the unlucky Alain Prost by just two points.

The Brabham team was on the slide, so at the end of 1985 Piquet decided to join the resurgent Williams team. During 1986, he established a bitter rivalry with teammate Nigel Mansell, who won five races to Piquet's four to lead the Championship going into the final race. In the end, tyre issues put paid to both drivers' ambitions, allowing Prost to sneak in and win the title.

Piquet was in remarkable form in 1987, securing nine consecutive podiums (including three wins) to secure his third and final World Championship. The Brazilian's victory in the driver' standings was even more remarkable, given that teammate Mansell won six races. It was typical of Piquet, a man who could come out top even when he was out-paced by his closest rivals.

Piquet enjoyed something of a career renaissance following his move to the new Benetton team in 1990, finishing third in the World Championship.

WILLIAMS & McLAREN

The McLaren team was the dominant force in Formula 1 during the early 1980s, with Niki Lauda (pictured) helping the team to collect a Drivers and Constructors Championship double in 1984.

The 1980s was a time of great change in Formula 1. This was most apparent at the front of the grid, where a new breed of teams headed by knowledgeable designers and engineers replaced once dominant outfits such as Brabham, Lotus and Ferrari. One era was over, and a new one was beginning.

The two teams who stepped up to the plate were McLaren and Williams. The former were hardly new to Formula 1, having first raced in 1966 and enjoyed Constructors Championship success in 1974. However, the installation of a brand new management team in 1981, headed by Ron Dennis, saw them surge to the front of the grid once more.

Williams, on the other hand, was a much newer proposition. The team was founded in 1977 by Frank Williams, a former driver and mechanic who had previously run a couple of unsuccessful Formula 1 outfits. Although it wasn't an immediate success, Williams secured its first Constructors Championship in 1980, with Alan Jones also securing the Drivers Championship. The team repeated the "double" in 1987, with Nelson Piquet taking the Drivers' crown.

When McLaren scooped the 1984 Constructors Championship, with returning Formula 1 great Niki Lauda winning the Drivers Championship, it set in motion a rivalry between the two teams that would last into the 1990s. Over the next decade, no other teams got close: between them, Williams and McLaren won every Constructors Championship from 1984 to 1994.

With such dominance, it was unsurprising that their drivers also thrived. During this decade of dominance McLaren drivers won the World Championship seven times, with Williams' drivers notching up three wins. In the 1988 season, McLaren's two drivers – Alain Prost and Ayrton Senna – won all but one race between them. In the end, it took a very special combination to end the Williams-McLaren era of dominance: Ferrari and Michael Schumacher.

Up to the mid 1990s, scenes like this duel between Ayrton Senna's McLaren and Nigel Mansell's Williams became a familiar sight at Formula 1 races.

KEKE
ROSBERG

During his peak in the early 1980s, Keke Rosberg lived up to his "Flying Finn" nickname. Even when driving underpowered cars, he was impressively quick, eking every inch of pace from his Williams in 1982 to become Finland's first World Champion.

Rosberg's 1982 Championship winning season was particularly sweet, given how hard he had to work to achieve it. It came almost a decade after he signalled his talent by winning the 1973 European Karting Championship. He then turned to Formula Vee, but by 1978 had hit something of a brick wall. Fiercely determined to succeed, in 1978 he raced in European Formula 2, and both the Formula Atlantic and Formula Pacific series. That season, he completed a staggering 41 races on 36 weekends.

It was a workload that would have overwhelmed most drivers, but it earned Rosberg a route into Formula 1. He was snapped up by the unfancied Theodore team and subsequently claimed his first victory in only his second race, the non-championship International Trophy Race at Silverstone. That a rookie could win in wet, windswept conditions marked him out as a driver to watch.

Things didn't go to plan, though. Hopping between the uncompetitive Theodore, ATS and Wolf teams, Rosberg often struggled even to qualify for races. He moved to the short-lived Fittipaldi team in 1980, but things barely improved, though he did score a memorable podium finish at the Argentinian Grand Prix. It seemed his Formula 1 career would peter out like so many others before him.

However, fate was smiling on the Flying Finn. After the collapse of the Fittipaldi team in 1981 he was given a chance to test drive a Williams following the retirement of 1980 World Champion Alan Jones. He grasped the opportunity with both hands.

Rosberg was scintillatingly fast in testing and Team Principal Frank Williams was impressed enough to offer him a contract for the 1982 season. The Williams car was competitive, giving the hard-working Finn the opportunity to show his class.

The 1982 season was an odd one in many ways, with 11 different drivers claiming Grand Prix victories. Rosberg won only once – in Switzerland at the end of August – but proved the most consistent driver over the course of the season. He was disqualified in Brazil and was forced to retire twice, but otherwise never finished outside of the top eight. In the end, it was this consistency and a quintet of podium finishes that earned him the World Championship.

Rosberg's Williams was rarely the fastest car on the grid, being severely underpowered compared to the new turbo engine cars. However, it was one of the most reliable, and in the end Rosberg was a worthy champion.

Much was expected of Keke Rosberg during his one season with McLaren (1986), but he struggled with an unreliable car and could only finish sixth in the World Championship.

STATISTICS

BORN	6th December 1948
NATIONALITY	Finnish
ACTIVE YEARS	1979–86
TEAMS	Theodore, ATS, Wolf, Fittipaldi, Williams, McLaren
TOTAL RACES	128 (114 starts)
WINS	5
PODIUM FINISHES	17
POLE POSITIONS	5
FIRST WIN	1982 Swiss Grand Prix
LAST WIN	1985 Australian Grand Prix
LAST RACE	1986 Australian Grand Prix

On his day, the "Flying Finn" was unstoppable. Unfortunately, those moments of greatness were few and far between; Rosberg won just five races throughout his nine-year Formula 1 career.

Keke Rosberg's 1985 season got off to the worst possible start. Hours after this picture was taken, he was forced to retire from the season-opening Brazilian Grand Prix.

Rosberg's career largely failed to ignite after this impressive triumph. With turbo-powered cars dominating the 1983 season, he was forced to settle for fifth place in the World Championship. He did manage a famous victory in Monaco, but it was scant consolation. It was a similar story in 1984, but he showed glimpses of his Championship-winning form in 1985, finally finishing third in the drivers' standings.

Big things were expected in 1986 following a move to McLaren but Rosberg was unable to keep pace with Alain Prost despite driving a faster car.

Rosberg retired at the end of the season, later turning his attention to management. He guided the careers of a string of drivers including JJ Lehto, two-time World Champion Mikka Hakkinnen and his own son Nico. When the latter won in Monaco in 2013, he became the first son of a former winner to win what is considered the sport's most iconic Grand Prix.

ALAIN
PROST

By anyone's standards, Alain Prost was a remarkable driver. It is not only his four World Championship wins that make him one of Formula 1's all-time greats but also his relaxed driving style – modelled on his heroes Jim Clark and Jackie Stewart – and his ability to successfully set up his car to make the most of the conditions. Controversy dogged him throughout his career but he was no temperamental hot head; in fact, his intelligence and calculating persona earned him the nickname "The Professor".

This calculating streak made Prost a difficult person for many Formula 1 fans to warm to, despite his immense driving ability. Like Schumacher and Vettel in later years, he always seemed in control. His bitter rivalries with more popular drivers – most notably the more artistic and exciting Ayrton Senna – earned him few fans. At his best, though, he was masterful, as his back-to-back titles in 1985 and 1986 proved.

After excelling in karting, Formula Renault and Formula 3, where he won both the French and European Championships, he was a man in demand in 1979. He was offered a drive by McLaren at the United States Grand Prix in 1979, but turned it down, saying he wasn't ready. He eventually signed for the team in 1980, enjoying a mixed debut season before controversially breaking his contract in order to sign with Renault.

He came close to winning the World Championship in 1982 and 1983, on the latter occasion finishing the season just behind Nelson Piquet. His failure to win infuriated his Renault employees, who set fire to his car outside his home. He moved his family to Switzerland and rejoined McLaren in 1984, again finishing runner up in the World Championship – this time to teammate Niki Lauda – by a mere half a point, the slimmest margin in Formula 1 history.

When things were going well, Alain Prost was all smiles, but when things went wrong he could be angry and temperamental.

STATISTICS

BORN	24th February 1955
NATIONALITY	French
ACTIVE YEARS	1980–91, 1993
TEAMS	McLaren, Renault, Ferrari, Williams
TOTAL RACES	202 (199 starts)
WINS	51
PODIUM FINISHES	106
POLE POSITIONS	33
FIRST WIN	1981 French Grand Prix
LAST WIN	1993 German Grand Prix
LAST RACE	1993 Australian Grand Prix

Alain Prost delighted his home fans by winning the 1989 French Grand Prix, one of four victories in his third World Championship winning season.

Prost sits in his Mclaren MP4/5 during practice for the 1989 Brazilian Grand Prix, a race in which he finished second to Ferrari's Nigel Mansell.

Prost subsequently dominated the next two seasons, becoming the first back-to-back champion since Jack Brabham in 1960. He was fortunate to be driving the McLaren MP4/2, the fastest and most reliable car of the period, but made the most of his opportunity in devastating fashion.

After surpassing Jackie Stewart's record for the greatest number of Grand Prix victories in 1987, he entered the 1988 season as the man to beat. This time, though, he would have a serious rival: new teammate Ayrton Senna.

The duo's battles on and off the track would become legendary. The pair won all but one of the World Championship races that season, with the Brazilian edging out the two-time champion to win his first title. Prost and Senna continued their heated battle the following season, but this time the Frenchman would prevail. However, The Professor courted controversy by forcing his rival off the track at the final race of the season, at Suzuka in Japan, to secure the title.

With the rivalry at breaking point, Prost moved to Ferrari for the 1990 season. Once again, he faced Senna in a final race eliminator in Japan. This time, Senna forced Prost off the track to claim the World Championship. It was a dramatic end to another nail-biting season.

After a poor season in 1991, Prost took a year off, returning in 1993 with the Williams team. He'd lost none of his skills during his break from racing, and stormed to seven wins and a fourth World Championship. It would be his last triumph. When Williams announced the signing of Senna for 1994, Prost quit, bowing out at the 1993 Australian Grand Prix with a second place finish. He retired with a career total of 51 race wins.

PROST vs SENNA

F ew Formula 1 rivalries have caught the public's imagination quite like the titanic tussles between Alain Prost and Ayrton Senna. Like the Hunt-Lauda rivalry before, it pitched two contrasting personalities head-to-head in an ongoing battle for World Championship domination.

Prost and Senna's rivalry was intensified by the fact that they were teammates, at least during the first two years of their six-year feud. When McLaren brought them together in 1988, Prost was a two-time World Champion; the controlled, model professional whose tactical and technical acumen was unsurpassed. Senna, on the other hand, was pure excitement – a driver with bags of talent who raced hard and was prone to losing his temper. It was a mixture that would guarantee fireworks.

The pair dominated the 1988 season, winning all but one race between them. Surprisingly – and much to Prost's annoyance – it was Senna who came out on top. It was merely a taste of what was to come.

In 1989, the pair's battles on and off the track became the stuff of legend. Matters came to a head at the season-ending Japanese Grand Prix, where Prost turned in on his teammate at the chicane, forcing him off the track. Senna was later disqualified for using the chicane's escape road, handing Prost the title.

Senna, never a man to forget a grudge, took his revenge a year later, crashing into Prost – now driving for Ferrari – on the first corner in Japan to secure his second World Championship. Prost was naturally furious, calling Senna "a man without value".

The pair never patched up their differences. Following Senna's death at the 1994 San Marino Grand Prix, Prost told reporters that he felt that "a part of me has died also". It was a poignant and honest tribute; in reality, Prost and Senna needed each other. It was their intense rivalry that spurred both men on to Formula 1 greatness.

Prost and Senna's relationship was more cordial following Prost's switch to Ferrari for the 1990 season. They were even able to share jokes on the podium, as shown here at the 1990 United States Grand Prix.

(inset): Prost and Senna's on-track battles became legendary particularly during their years together at McLaren.

1990s

AYRTON SENNA

Ayrton Senna looks pensive ahead of the 1994 Brazilian Grand Prix. A few weeks later, he lost his life at the San Marino Grand Prix.

Few who saw Ayrton Senna race would argue that the man had immense talent. In fact, many observers still believe that he was the most talented driver ever to grace Formula 1. Certainly, he was one of the fastest, his record of 65 pole positions is a lasting testament to his raw speed. The three-time World Champion's death, following a brutal crash at the 1994 San Marino Grand Prix, cast a long shadow over the sport, and led to scenes of national mourning in his native Brazil.

When Senna was behind the wheel of a Formula 1 car, excitement was never far away. He had an unshakeable will to win at all costs, and drove each race as if it could be his last. He regularly fell out with teammates – most notably Alain Prost during their shared years at McLaren in the 1980s – and fellow drivers, once famously punching Eddie Irvine in the face following an on-track altercation at the 1993 Japanese Grand Prix.

His obsession with speed bordered on recklessness. Yet more often than not, his risky overtaking moves and "pedal to the metal" approach paid off. This made him hugely popular with fans, and one of the best all-round drivers Formula 1 has ever seen.

Senna first got into a kart aged four, and was winning races by the age of 13. By the time he was 17 years old, he was South American Karting Champion and one of the most hotly tipped drivers on the World Karting Championship circuit. A move to Britain in 1981 resulted in a Formula Ford Championship win. After spending a couple of years back in Brazil at his family's request, he returned to Europe in 1983 to win the British Formula 3 Championship. This made Senna a hot property, and after Formula 1 test drives with Williams, McLaren and Brabham, Senna chose to join the relatively unknown Toleman team.

STATISTICS

BORN	21st March 1960
NATIONALITY	Brazilian
ACTIVE YEARS	1984–94
TEAMS	Toleman, Lotus, McLaren, Williams
TOTAL RACES	162 (161 starts)
WINS	41
PODIUM FINISHES	80
POLE POSITIONS	65
FIRST WIN	1985 Portuguese Grand Prix
LAST WIN	1993 Australian Grand Prix
LAST RACE	1994 San Marino Grand Prix

When his Williams car crashed at Imola in Italy, Ayrton Senna sustained serious head injuries from which he would never recover.

Senna's early years in Formula 1 – first with Toleman and later Lotus, which he joined in 1985 – were largely unspectacular but there were plenty of signs of his immense talent. He finished second at Monaco in his debut season, and secured his first win at the 1985 Portuguese Grand Prix. Five more wins and 16 podium finishes over the next two seasons saw his stock rise, and in 1988, Senna teamed up with Alain Prost at McLaren.

Behind the wheel of the fastest and most competitive car on the grid, Senna began to show his class. After being disqualified in the season-opening Brazilian Grand Prix, he went on to win eight of the remaining 15 races to out-score teammate Prost and secure a first World Championship.

Senna's relationship with Prost soured further in 1989, culminating in the famous final-race World Championship showdown at Suzuka in Japan. Prost forced Senna off the track, and Senna was disqualified for using the chicane's escape road, handing the title to the Frenchman. Senna duly took his revenge the following season, crashing into Prost early on to send both drivers out of the race and for Senna to regain the World Championship.

With Prost out of the picture in 1991, Senna's main rival was Briton Nigel Mansell. The two went toe-to-toe throughout the season, with Mansell matching Senna for speed. It was Senna who prevailed, though, securing his third and final World Championship.

With McLaren on the wane Senna angled for a move to Williams in 1993, only to be blocked by the team's lead driver: Alain Prost. When the Frenchman retired at the end of 1993, Senna switched to Williams. It would be his last move in Formula 1. At the third race of the 1994 season in San Marino, his car veered off the track and hit a concrete wall. It was a tragic end to one of Formula 1's most remarkable careers.

Senna looked agitated before the 1990 Japanese Grand Prix. In the end, his crash with his rival, Alain Prost, would secure him the World Championship.

NIGEL
MANSELL

Nigel Mansell had a reputation, perhaps unfairly, for being one of Formula 1's less colourful characters off the track. When he was behind the wheel of a racing car, however, Mansell was a man transformed. He drove fast, had a reputation for making bold overtaking moves and was exciting to watch.

Mansell's path to becoming 1992 World Champion was far from easy. By the time he arrived in Formula 1 he was something of a grizzled veteran, having funded his way through the lower formulae. Along the way, he spent plenty of time on the sidelines recovering from heavy crashes. Somehow, his will to make it in Formula 1 never wavered.

This was amply demonstrated when he was finally offered a test drive for Lotus in 1980. He drove with several broken vertebrae following a crash in a Formula 3 race – injuries he hid from Lotus – and impressed enough to be signed as the team's test driver. He made his Formula 1 debut at the Austrian Grand Prix, and showed his steely determination by driving for most of the race with first and second degree burns on his backside following a fuel leak.

The unsuccessful period Mansell endured at Lotus would have finished off the careers of many lesser drivers but the Briton was made of sterner stuff. After a decent first season with Williams in 1985, he found himself amongst the World Championship contenders in 1986. If he had finished third at the final Grand Prix of the season in Australia he would have won the Championship; in the end, his chances were dashed by a tyre blow-out with 19 laps to go.

Mansell excelled in 1987 and once again he finished runner-up in the Championship. A couple of disappointing seasons followed, and Mansell made a surprise move to Ferrari in 1989. A fourth-place finish in the drivers' standings showed the potential of the partnership but things began to unravel upon the arrival of Alan Prost as teammate in 1990. Prost would not accept a fair fight with Mansell, and the Briton became so disillusioned that he announced his retirement.

Frank Williams persuaded him to reconsider and in 1991, he rejoined the British team. Driving one of the fastest cars on the grid, Mansell was again amongst the points, claiming five victories to finish runner-up to Senna.

Mansell's move to Ferrari in 1989 thrilled the team's passionate fan base, who nicknamed him "Il Leone" (The Lion) for his fearless driving style.

It was a different story in 1992. Behind the wheel of a dominant car, Mansell ran away with the Championship. He won the first five races of the season and nine in total, picking up 14 pole positions in the process. It made him the most successful British driver in terms of race victories (a record previously held by Jackie Stewart). More importantly, he was finally World Champion.

Surprisingly, he was forced out of Williams by the arrival of Alain Prost – a man he'd refused to work with again following his experience at Ferrari – at the tail end of 1992, and promptly retired from Formula 1. Instead, he headed to the US IndyCar circuit, winning the 1993 CART Championship. He made a brief return to Formula 1 in 1994 but finally called it a day in 1995.

STATISTICS

BORN	8th August 1953
NATIONALITY	British
ACTIVE YEARS	1980–92, 1994–95
TEAMS	Lotus, Williams, Ferrari, McLaren
TOTAL RACES	191 (187 starts)
WINS	31
PODIUM FINISHES	59
POLE POSITIONS	32
FIRST WIN	1985 European Grand Prix
LAST WIN	1994 Australian Grand Prix
LAST RACE	1995 Spanish Grand Prix

Mansell's laidback public persona hid a man who was prone to wild mood swings off the track.

Nigel Mansell was fearless
behind the wheel of a Formula 1
car and enjoyed success at every
team he joined. Only the presence
of all-time greats on the grid denied
him more World Championships.

DAMON HILL

By the time he joined the Jordan team in 1998, Damon Hill was a shadow of his former self but he continued to give everything to improve the fortunes of Eddie Jordan's team.

Frank Williams once called Damon Hill a "tough bastard", something of a compliment in the cutthroat world of Formula 1. Hill is renowned for being a nice guy off the track, yet this easy-going exterior hides determination and a fearsome will to succeed. Hill needed both of these qualities to make his way in motor racing, despite the recognition his famous surname – and even more famous father – brought. The fact that he became a deserving World Champion in 1996 is testament to his fighting qualities.

Hill was 15 years old when his father, Graham – himself a two-time World Champion – was killed in a plane crash. With no fat inheritance to fritter away on racing and partying, he was forced to go out to work to support his mother and sisters. He worked on building sites before landing a job as a motorcycle courier, which in turn led him to begin a career in amateur motorbike racing at the late age of 21.

Hill switched from two wheels to four on his mother's advice, and began a long apprenticeship in car racing. His first full season came in 1985, where he won six races in the British Formula Ford Championship. He later switched to Formula 3 and Formula 3000, showing glimpses of his true future potential.

Any dreams of following in his father's footsteps still seemed far-fetched, until Frank Williams offered him a spot as a Formula 1 test driver in 1991, ten years after his first motorcycle race. Hill took a chance signing with the declining Brabham team for the 1992 season but struggled with a poor car. Luckily, he continued to enjoy a good relationship with Williams and was offered a place on the team for the 1993 season, as partner to the returning Alain Prost.

Damon Hill endured a horrific World Championship title defence with Arrows in 1997, scoring just seven points.

STATISTICS

BORN	17th September 1960
NATIONALITY	British
ACTIVE YEARS	1992–99
TEAMS	Brabham, Williams, Arrows, Jordan
TOTAL RACES	122 (115 starts)
WINS	22
PODIUM FINISHES	42
POLE POSITIONS	20
FIRST WIN	1993 Hungarian Grand Prix
LAST WIN	1998 Belgian Grand Prix
LAST RACE	1999 Japanese Grand Prix

Hill performed admirably in his first full season with Williams, getting on with the notoriously picky Prost and securing some excellent results. He grabbed his first Formula 1 win, aged 33 years, at the Hungarian Grand Prix and followed it up with two more victories and a third place finish in the World Championship.

In 1994, he retained his place on the team, this time alongside Ayrton Senna. The Brazilian's tragic death three races into the season thrust Hill into the limelight for the first time, and he responded brilliantly. He won six races that season and went into the final Grand Prix of the year in Australia neck and neck with Benetton's fast-rising superstar, Michael Schumacher, at the top of the drivers' standings. In another controversial Formula 1 finish, Schumacher crashed into Hill when the latter appeared to be making a decisive overtaking move, denying the Briton his first World Championship.

The two would continue to battle for supremacy over the coming seasons. Schumacher came out top in 1995 but in 1996, with the German hampered by an unreliable Ferrari, Hill was the man to beat. It wasn't plain sailing, with junior teammate Jacques Villeneuve, proving more than a match for the veteran Briton in the second half of the season but Hill ultimately claimed the prize he'd been chasing for 15 years. In the process, he became the first son of a Formula 1 World Champion to also win the title.

Hill acrimoniously parted company with Williams at the end of the season – the decision to replace him having been taken a year earlier – and joined the tiny Arrows team. He endured a dismal year in a poor car, scoring just seven points in the 1997 season. A move to Jordan proved a little more successful, but a poor run of form in 1999 forced him to retire, just three years after his greatest triumph.

Damon Hill's friendly demeanour and sporting nature hid a battle-hardened professional who was determined to make the most of his time in Formula 1.

JACQUES VILLENEUVE

Jacques Villeneuve was just 11 years old when his father, one of the sport's greatest talents, Gilles, was killed in a crash in 1982. Far from putting Jacques off striving for a career in Formula 1, it made the youngster even more determined to succeed.

The Canadian enjoyed a prodigious rise through the racing ranks, succeeding in the Italian and Japanese Formula 3 championships before heading to the United States in 1993 to join the Formula Atlantic Championship. A third-place finish secured him a drive in the IndyCar World Series for 1994 and the Rookie of the Year prize. In 1995, he followed it up with a Drivers Championship.

With such credentials and a famous surname, it was no surprise when Williams offered him a drive for the 1996 season, partnering Damon Hill. Villeneuve proved an instant hit, pushing Hill all the way.

With Hill out of the picture in 1997, Villeneuve battled with Michael Schumacher, now getting the best out of his Ferrari, for the World Championship. The Canadian trailed Schumacher by a single point going into the final race of the season in Jerez, Spain. In the closing stages of a thrilling Grand Prix, Schumacher turned into the overtaking Villeneuve. Despite this, Villeneuve went on to claim third place and the Championship, while Schumacher was disqualified for causing an avoidable accident.

Villeneuve continued racing in Formula 1 until 2006 but further success eluded him. He retired having secured the Villeneuve name in the pantheon of Formula 1 champions, a feat his talented father never achieved.

Jacques Villeneuve is pictured at the Gilles Villeneuve Circuit in Montreal, a track named after his late father, who was a Formula 1 star in the early 1980s.

STATISTICS

BORN	9th April 1971
NATIONALITY	Canadian
ACTIVE YEARS	1996–2006
TEAMS	Williams, BAR, Renault, Sauber, BMW Sauber
TOTAL RACES	165 (164 starts)
WINS	11
PODIUM FINISHES	23
POLE POSITIONS	13
FIRST WIN	1996 European Grand Prix
LAST WIN	1997 Luxemburg Grand Prix
LAST RACE	2006 German Grand Prix

Jacques Villeneuve was unable to mount any kind of title challenge during his final year in Formula 1, which he spent driving a poor BMW Sauber.

THE RETURN OF THE PRANCING HORSE

The Ferrari name has been synonymous with Formula 1 since the sport's birth. To date, the Italian team has competed in each of the sport's 64 World Championships, scooping 16 Constructors Championships and 15 Drivers Championships.

Today, we think of Scuderia Ferrari as consistent challengers as they had been in the earliest years of the sport, under the stewardship of founder Enzo Ferrari. They may not always win but they are there or thereabouts, producing competitive cars driven by talented drivers for their legion of fans to cheer on.

For all their history and success, Ferrari has not always been Formula 1 frontrunners. The rise of McLaren and Williams during the 1980s sent the Italian team into a downward spiral, from which many thought they would never recover. Where other teams saw new regulations and engine sizes as an opportunity, Ferrari's owners railed against the changes. Fundamentally, they were living off past glories.

By 1996, they had not won the Constructors Championship for 13 years, and their last Drivers title was back in 1979. Clearly, something had to be done. Rolling the dice, they recruited the nucleus of the wildly successful Benetton team – two-time World Champion Michael Schumacher, technical director Ross Brawn and chief designer Rory Byrne. It was a masterstroke.

The trio changed the car significantly, ditching Ferrari's traditional V12 engine for a slimline V12. Over the next three years, Schumacher, Brawn and Byrne worked tirelessly, with results improving year-on-year. The Constructors Championship was secured in 1999, with Schumacher adding the drivers' title a year later.

Three more titles followed in quick succession, as the relentless German and the Italian team dominated. Races became a procession, with other teams struggling to replicate the pace and reliability of Brawn and Byrne's Ferrari. After years in the wilderness, the Prancing Horse was back where it belonged.

Together with key technical staff poached from Benetton, Eddie Irvine (left) and Michael Schumacher masterminded the resurgence of Ferrari in the late 1990s.

Few were more passionate about Formula 1 than the late, great Enzo Ferrari, whose team had fallen into sharp decline at the time of his death in 1988.

MIKA
HAKKINEN

During the early years of his career, Mika Hakkinen was managed by former Formula 1 World Champion and fellow Finn, Keke Rosberg.

Had Mika Hakkinen not received emergency medical treatment following a crash in practice at the 1995 Australian Grand Prix in Adelaide, his name may well have become another to add to Formula 1's list of drivers killed in action. Remarkably, the popular Finn battled back from this setback to claim back-to-back World Championship titles in 1998 and 1999.

Almost as remarkably, Hakkinen won both titles by beating Michael Schumacher at the height of his Ferrari pomp. The two drivers were old rivals, having first clashed in Formula 3 in 1990 during their ascent to Formula 1. Schumacher, not for the last time, denied a rival a race win by making contact with his car.

By this point, Hakkinen was well on his way to securing a drive in Formula 1. He'd already won five karting championships by the time he turned 18, and his 1990 British Formula 3 title was enough to secure a contract with the ailing Lotus team. Hakkinen was dogged with technical issues throughout his time with the once great British outfit and it was only when he joined McLaren in 1993, that things finally began to look up.

To begin with, Hakkinen had to make do with being a test driver but eventually, his chance came. On his debut, at the 1993 Portuguese Grand Prix, he out-qualified team mate Ayrton Senna. Then, at the next race in Japan, he secured his first podium finish. With Senna leaving for Williams, it was enough to secure Hakkinen the team leader's seat for 1994. He impressed with six podium finishes to end the season fourth in the World Championship standings but McLaren expected more.

In 1999, Mika Hakkinen became the seventh driver to win back-to-back World Championships.

STATISTICS

BORN	28th September 1968
NATIONALITY	Finnish
ACTIVE YEARS	1991–2001
TEAMS	Lotus, McLaren
TOTAL RACES	165 (161 starts)
WINS	20
PODIUM FINISHES	51
POLE POSITIONS	26
FIRST WIN	1997 European Grand Prix
LAST WIN	2001 United States Grand Prix
LAST RACE	2001 Japanese Grand Prix

A number of mediocre seasons with McLaren followed, as Hakkinen had to settle for occasional podiums and plenty of point-scoring finishes. Having still not won a Grand Prix, there were whispers around the paddock about his long-term future in the sport.

Once that first win came – at the European Grand Prix at Jerez, Spain, in 1997 – Hakkinen was a changed driver. He got off to a flying start in 1998, winning the season-opening Australian Grand Prix in Melbourne to set down a marker to the rest of the field. In the end, his only challenge came from old rival Michael Schumacher. By the end of the season, Hakkinen's eight wins and 11 podium finishes were enough to hold off the German's charge.

The following year, cracks began to appear in Hakkinen's previously unflappable façade. With Schumacher recovering from a broken leg, it was the German's Ferrari teammate, Eddie Irvine, who emerged as the greatest threat to his crown. The Irishman pushed him all the way and Hakkinen showed signs of wilting under pressure when he broke down crying after spinning off at the Italian Grand Prix. It was merely a blip; Hakkinen won a final race Championship decider in Japan to claim back-to-back World Championships.

Old rival Michael Schumacher roared back in 2000 and despite four wins and 11 podium finishes, Hakkinen had to settle for second place. Ferrari was dominant, and the previously front-running McLaren team had to play catch-up. Sadly, they simply couldn't do it. After a disappointing 2001 season where he recorded just two wins – including a final hurrah at the United States Grand Prix, where he got the better of old foe Michael Schumacher one last time – Hakkinen decide to retire. By then, his place among the greats of Formula 1 had already been assured.

Mika Hakkinen celebrates winning the 2000 Austrian Grand Prix, the 16th victory of his illustrious career.

THE MODERN ERA
2000-PRESENT DAY

MICHAEL
SCHUMACHER

Michael Schumacher knew what he wanted, and did everything he could to achieve it. Achieve it he did, when he quit Formula 1 in 2012 after 21 years in the sport, he'd notched up a record breaking 91 wins in 308 races, a win ratio that brought him seven World Championship titles, three more than any other Formula 1 driver.

Although Schumacher's story has an uncertain ending following his life-threatening skiing crash in December 2013, his fighting qualities are such that few would be surprised if he made a miraculous recovery.

Faced with adversity, Schumacher has nearly always come out on top. His desire to win was so strong during his Formula 1 career that he wasn't averse to forcing rivals wide or even crashing into them to achieve his goals. Twice, World Championship campaigns were decided by Schumacher's aggressive tactics against his nearest rivals; in 1994, his crash with Damon Hill secured his first Drivers Championship, while in 1997 he fell foul of race stewards after driving into Jacques Villeneuve, who subsequently took the title.

For all the controversy, for the most part Schumacher was simply better than his rivals. Like Niki Lauda before him, the legendary German knew how to set up a car. He built up relationships with engineers, designers and mechanics – most notably Benetton and Ferrari technical director Ross Brawn – and played a vital role in developing cars in which he could win. Once the car was perfected, he was unstoppable.

The first time Schumacher did this was with Flavio Briatore's Benetton team of the early 1990s. Having secured a place in the team on the strength of a handful of drives for Jordan in 1991 – not to mention an impressive track record in karting, Formula 3 and F3000 – he began making his mark in 1992.

Michael Schumacher drastically turned around the fortunes of the ailing Ferrari team, winning five World Championships in the team's famous racing colours.

STATISTICS

BORN	3rd January 1969
NATIONALITY	German
ACTIVE YEARS	1991–2006, 2010–12
TEAMS	Jordan, Benetton, Ferrari, Mercedes
TOTAL RACES	308 (307 starts)
WINS	91
PODIUM FINISHES	155
POLE POSITIONS	68
FIRST WIN	1992 Belgian Grand Prix
LAST WIN	2006 Chinese Grand Prix
LAST RACE	2012 Brazilian Grand Prix

Michael Schumacher showed signs of greatness during his first year in Formula 1 with Benetton in 1992; within two years he would be World Champion.

By his standards, the 2003 season was a disappointing one for Michael Schumacher. He tasted victory only six times, though it was enough to secure yet another World Championship.

Schumacher secured his first win at the 1992 Belgian Grand Prix and a further seven podium finishes saw him claim third place in the Drivers Championship. From then on, it just got better. Having finally perfected the Ford-powered Benetton in 1994, he edged out Williams' Damon Hill to claim his first World Championship. Schumacher repeated the feat a year later, this time driving his Benetton-Renault to nine Grand Prix victories as he ran away with the title.

A big-money move to the ailing Ferrari team followed, with key technical staff Ross Brawn and Rory Byrne joining Schumacher at the famous Italian marque. They were competitive immediately but it would take until 2000, for the trio to perfect the formula for success. Once they did, nobody could touch them. Schumacher claimed five consecutive World Championship titles from 2000 to 2004, dominating the sport like no driver before or since.

Even now, the statistics are remarkable. During the 2004 season, Schumacher won 13 of the year's 18 races, giving him an astonishing win ratio of 73 per cent. He failed to reach the podium on only three occasions. Ferrari's dominance was such that Schumacher's teammate, Rubens Barrichello, was his closest rival.

Schumacher decided to call it a day at the end of the 2006 season with a bulging list of Formula 1 records to his name – many of which may never be broken. However, he was tempted out of retirement by the rebirth of the Mercedes team in 2010. Making the long-dormant German giants great again clearly appealed to his romantic side, but the car's uncompetitive nature hampered Schumacher's chances. After three seasons battling it out for places in midfield, he finally retired for good in 2012, his place atop the list of Formula 1 greats long since assured.

FERNANDO ALONSO

Fernando Alonso has become as famous for his off-track tantrums as his metronomic consistency on it.

When he won his first World Championship in 2005, aged just 24, many in Formula 1 thought that Fernando Alonso would go on to dominate Formula 1, just as Michael Schumacher had done before him. The fact that Alonso has added just one more Drivers Championship to his CV – and that was in 2006 – is a source of constant frustration to the Spaniard.

In an era packed with talented drivers, Alonso is widely regarded as the best of his generation. "I might not be the fastest, or the most technical," he was once quoted as saying, "but I am the most consistent." It's this consistency that's seen him pick up wins in all but four of his 13 seasons in Formula 1 and Championship challenger on only a handful of occasions.

For all his consistency, Alonso has flaws. He's rarely been a team player and has been forced to change teams several times, in order to be the undisputed top dog. His move to McLaren for the 2007 season seemed a good choice at the time, but quickly fell apart when he was out-paced and out-scored by young teammate Lewis Hamilton. It's a rivalry that has only intensified over the years, despite both drivers' struggles to match the pace and consistency of Sebastian Vettel in recent years.

Alonso's rise to Formula 1 champion was meteoric, to say the least. He claimed a World Karting Championship as a teenager, before moving to the Euro Open Championship with Nissan in 1999 (a title he subsequently added to his resume at the first attempt). His exploits in F3000 – the forerunner to today's GP2 Championship – earned him a test drive with Minardi, and a move to Formula 1 racing in 2001.

Alonso performed admirably in his first season with Renault in 2003. In 2005, he delivered the French manufacturer's first Drivers Championship.

STATISTICS*

BORN	29th July 1981
NATIONALITY	Spanish
ACTIVE YEARS	2001–present
TEAMS	Minardi, Renault, McLaren, Ferrari
TOTAL RACES	220 (219 starts)
WINS	32
PODIUM FINISHES	95
POLE POSITIONS	22
FIRST WIN	2003 Hungarian Grand Prix
LAST WIN	2013 Spanish Grand Prix
LAST RACE	–

*Statistics correct as of May 2016

After a season impressing in an uncompetitive car, Alonso moved to Renault in 2002 to be the team's designated test driver. He was rewarded with a place on the French manufacturer's Formula 1 team in 2003. Alonso wasted no time in making his mark, winning the Hungarian Grand Prix a few months later.

A consistent, if underwhelming, season followed in 2004, as Alonso struggled to keep pace with the dominant Ferraris at the front of the grid. Everything came together in 2005, though, when Alonso surged to seven race wins on the way to his first World Championship ahead of McLaren's Kimi Räikkönen. In the process, he ended the five-year dominance of Ferrari's Michael Schumacher.

Impressively, Alonso retained his title in 2006, once again proving the most consistent driver on the grid. He won six of the first nine races to establish a dominant lead in the Drivers Championship but was forced to hold off a late charge from Michael Schumacher. Alonso showed little sign of feeling the pressure at the penultimate Grand Prix of the season in Japan, finishing first to secure back-to-back Championships.

A nightmare year at McLaren followed, resulting in a swift return to Renault. Much to Alonso's frustration, he was unable to compete with the pace of former teammate Lewis Hamilton and Ferrari's Felipe Massa. Things were worse in 2009, as Renault struggled to compete, resulting in a high profile switch to Ferrari.

Since then, there have been notable highs and lows – his 2010 final-race Championship loss to Sebastian Vettel following a poor tyre strategy, being the most heartbreaking. Although he hasn't regained the title, given his consistency and fighting qualities, few would bet against Alonso adding another title to his resume in the coming years.

Alonso celebrates winning the 2005 Chinese Grand Prix at the Shanghai circuit, thus securing both the Constructors and Drivers World Championships.

KIMI RÄIKKÖNEN

In many respects, Kimi Räikkönen is a refreshing blast from the past. His playboy lifestyle, famously opulent salary and relaxed attitude to racing make him come across like a relic from Formula 1's halcyon days in the 1970s. It's this laidback approach and simplistic attitude – he was once quoted saying: "I never really think about what I'm doing, I just do it" – that makes him one of the most likeable drivers in Formula 1.

Famously, Räikkönen was notoriously laidback, horizontal, in fact, on the day he made his Formula 1 debut, driving for Sauber at the 2001 Australian Grand Prix. While other drivers went through their usual visualisation techniques and fretted about the set-up of their cars, the "Iceman" slept. He woke from his slumber 30 minutes before the race, wandered down to the pits, got in his car and was ready for the greatest moment of his career to date. Amazingly, he finished the race in sixth place, joining an elite group of drivers who have scored points on their Formula 1 debut.

Räikkönen had been marked out as a future Formula 1 champion from an early age, having progressed quickly through karting, Formula Ford and Formula Renault. In 2000, he won seven out of ten races to claim the Formula Reanult UK Championship. It was this impressive record that earned him a test drive with Sauber in September 2000, and subsequently a place on their Formula 1 team for 2001.

Nine points in Räikkönen's debut season was enough to secure him a move to McLaren, where he began to impress with a debut win at the 2003 Malaysian Grand Prix and the runner-up spot in the World Championship. He was Fernando Alonso's closest challenger in the 2005 season, finishing second in the World Championship with an impressive 112 points – a haul that equalled Alain Prost's 1984 record for a runner up.

Räikkönen is as well-known for his exploits and playboy lifestyle off the track as his impressive feats on it.

STATISTICS*

BORN	17th October 1979
NATIONALITY	Finnish
ACTIVE YEARS	2001–09, 2012–present
TEAMS	Sauber, McLaren, Lotus, Ferrari
TOTAL RACES	197 (196 starts)
WINS	20
PODIUM FINISHES	81
POLE POSITIONS	16
FIRST WIN	2003 Malaysian Grand Prix
LAST WIN	2013 Australian Grand Prix
LAST RACE	–

*Statistics correct as of May 2016

Kimi Räikkönen returned to Ferrari in 2014, five years after he won the World Championship with the famous Italian team.

At the 2012 Abu Dhabi Grand Prix, Kimi Räikkönen delivered Lotus its first victory since returning to the Formula 1 paddock.

Things didn't go quite so well for Räikkönen in 2006, where he fell foul of an unresponsive and underpowered McLaren. At the end of that season he joined Ferrari in a big money move. His salary was reported to be around $25 million a year, making him second only to Tiger Woods' in the global sports earnings charts.

His move to Ferrari was successful, with Räikkönen eventually beating Lewis Hamilton to the 2007 title by a single point at the final race of the season. He had to wait a month to celebrate his success, though, after a long, drawn-out investigation into fuel irregularities.

A couple of so-so seasons followed, before Ferrari announced the signing of Fernando Alonso – a man who refuses to play second fiddle to anyone – in September 2009. As Räikkönen had a year left on his contract, he left Ferrari with a $25 million pay-off.

Räikkönen didn't quit racing though, and he competed in the 2010 World Rally Championship before setting his sights on success in the US NASCAR series. He failed to find the success he craved, and began angling for a return to Formula 1. That eventually came in 2012, where he agreed terms with Lotus to become their lead driver. Räikkönen responded well to the challenge, winning the Abu Dhabi Grand Prix from fourth place on the grid and ending the season third in the Drivers Championship.

Another strong season at Lotus followed, giving him the chance to move to a bigger, stronger team for 2014. He was rumoured to be heading to Red Bull to replace Mark Webber but instead, ended up rejoining Ferrari as partner to two-time World Champion Fernando Alonso. Given the Spaniard's well-known need to be top dog, Räikkönen could spend what's left of his career playing second fiddle to a man he's often beaten on the track.

ALONSO vs HAMILTON

Formula 1 is no stranger to warring teammates but the 2007 feud between McLaren rivals, Fernando Alonso and Lewis Hamilton, was bitter even by motor sport standards. It had intrigue, controversy and echoes of the infamous spat between McLaren teammates Ayrton Senna and Alain Prost, which similarly dominated headlines between 1988 and 1989.

Alonso headed to McLaren in 2007 as the reigning double World Champion. His partner, meanwhile, was a hotly tipped rookie and one who had enjoyed a long relationship with McLaren, having signed to their driver development programme as a raw 13-year-old in 1998 – with no prior experience in Formula 1.

Alonso expected to be the team's designated leader but from the start was frustrated by McLaren's insistence that they would treat both drivers equally. They would simply let the pair race and not interfere. Hamilton quickly showed he was a match for the reigning World Champion and murmurs began to emerge from the paddock of Alonso's irritation with someone he viewed as a junior partner.

Matters came to a head at the Hungarian Grand Prix, the 11th race of the season. Alonso, desperate to claim pole position, blocked the pit box in the closing stages of qualifying, thus denying Hamilton a chance to change tyres and record a quicker time. Hamilton was furious and battle lines had been drawn. Race stewards subsequently gave Alonso a five-place grid penalty, thus handing Hamilton pole position. Hamilton won the race and went on to challenge for the title, while Alonso – still smarting from McLaren's refusal to prioritise him over Hamilton – endured a turbulent season.

Alonso had the last laugh, though, when an email exchange with fellow Spanish driver Pedro de la Rosa containing "stolen" Ferrari technical data, obtained by a McLaren engineer, was leaked to the media. As a result, the McLaren team was stripped of all of its 2007 Constructors points and Alonso's relationship with McLaren had been damaged beyond repair.

As reigning World Champion, Alonso found playing second fiddle to rookie driver Lewis Hamilton hard to take during the 2007 season. This muted celebration following the United States Grand Prix became a familiar sight that year.

The on-track rivalry between Lewis Hamilton (closest to the camera) and Fernando Alonso came to a head at the 2007 Hungarian Grand Prix.

LEWIS HAMILTON

By 2012, Lewis Hamilton's famously long and fruitful relationship with the McLaren team was beginning to sour. At the end of the season, he joined Mercedes in a big-money move.

There's rarely a dull moment when Lewis Hamilton is around. One of the most exciting and talented drivers of his generation, the Briton is never content settling for second place. While this fearless winning mentality was a huge factor in his astonishing rise to become the sport's youngest ever World Champion at the age of 23 (a record subsequently broken by Sebastian Vettel), it could be construed as something of a weakness, too. Many times Hamilton has been forced to retire from races after pushing his car just that little bit too hard, often after attempting daring overtaking moves that his rivals wouldn't even have considered.

Hamilton, like former teammate and bitter rival Fernando Alonso, has found life more difficult since claiming his solitary World Championship in 2008. He's struggled to regain that form, fallen out with the McLaren team that did so much to support his racing ambitions, and found himself in uncompetitive cars, watching as rival Sebastian

Vettel has driven away with title after title. That said, the dominance of his Mercedes team at the start of the 2014 season gives hope to the driven Briton that a second World Championship may not be that far away.

Hamilton's ascent to motorsport greatness is scarcely believable, even by Formula 1 standards. Encouraged by his father, Anthony, who worked long hours to help fund his son's racing ambitions, Hamilton began racing karts at the age of eight. By the time he was ten years old, he was British Champion. He famously approached McLaren team boss, Ron Dennis, at an awards ceremony to tell him that he'd like to drive for the Formula 1 outfit one day. Dennis was impressed; three years later he signed Hamilton to the team's Young Driver Support Programme. Hamilton repaid McLaren's faith by going on to win Championships in Formula Renault (2003), Formula 3 Euroseries (2005) and GP2 (2006).

Hamilton started the 2014 season in style, winning back-to-back races in Malaysia and Bahrain.

STATISTICS*

BORN	7th January 1985
NATIONALITY	British
ACTIVE YEARS	2007–present
TEAMS	McLaren, Mercedes
TOTAL RACES	170
WINS	43
PODIUM FINISHES	89
POLE POSITIONS	51
FIRST WIN	2007 Canadian Grand Prix
LAST WIN	2015 Austin Grand Prix
LAST RACE	–

*Statistics correct as of May 2016

By 2007, McLaren finally thought Hamilton was ready to make the step up to Formula 1. Partnering reigning World Champion, Fernando Alonso (a relationship that would quickly turn ugly), the young Briton enjoyed a sensational first year in Formula 1. He made the podium on each of his nine races – a staggering result for a Formula 1 rookie – and claimed his first race victory at the Canadian Grand Prix. He went on to miss out on what would have been a stunning debut World Championship by a single point, edged out in the final race of the season by Ferrari's Kimi Räikkönen.

With Alonso departing in a blaze of publicity at the end of the season, the coast was clear for Hamilton to make his mark in 2008. This he did in some style, heading into the final race of the season in Brazil seven points clear of nearest rival Felipe Massa at the top of the World Championship standings. Hamilton needed to finish fifth at worst to secure the Championship; he did it, but only after pulling off a brilliant last-gasp overtaking move on Timo Glock, in the closing stages of the race.

Since then, Hamilton's career has stumbled, with McLaren's inability to produce a car to rival that developed by Red Bull, a constant source of frustration. Few were surprised when he joined Mercedes for the start of the 2013 season. While that first season was only a moderate success, the German team's dominance in the opening races of 2014 suggests that Hamilton made the right decision.

Whether Hamilton adds further World Championship titles to his CV remains to be seen but there's little argument that he has the talent and ambition to do so. He's already won as many Grand Prix races as the great Juan Manuel Fangio; before his career is out, he may well be the most successful British driver of all time.

Lewis Hamilton enjoyed an amazing debut season in 2007, losing out on a first World Championship by a single point.

WHEN BRAWN BEAT THEM ALL

Ross Brawn was no stranger to Formula 1 success, having guided Benetton and Ferrari to multiple Drivers and Constructors World Championships throughout the 1990s and 2000s. Yet these achievements pale into insignificance when compared to what the experienced technical director and team principle achieved in 2009, when his Brawn GP team secured both the Drivers and Constructors Championships in their first – and only – season in Formula 1.

The team's success was remarkable given the circumstances of their formation. In 2008, Ross Brawn had joined the ailing Honda team with the proviso of making them competitive. Things did not go to plan early in the season so Brawn set about designing a car for the 2009 season earlier than their rivals. Then, out of the blue, Honda announced their withdrawal from Formula 1, leaving the team's future in doubt.

Brawn knew they had a car that could compete in 2009 – he'd studied the rule changes coming into the sport in fine detail, and had stolen a march on Honda's rivals – so he persuaded the Japanese manufacturer to sell him the team. The team's drivers, including Jenson Button, agreed pay-cuts to help the buyout go through. Finally, just weeks from the start of the 2009 season, the deal was completed and team Brawn GP was born.

Predictably, Brawn was proven right. Having perfected an aerodynamic feature called the "double diffuser" – something that would subsequently be banned from the sport from 2009 onwards – Brawn GP dominated the early rounds of the season, with Jenson Button winning six of the first seven races. While rival teams would ultimately catch-up, Brawn GP secured both the Constructors and Drivers Championships at the penultimate race of the season in Brazil, starting wild celebrations from a team whose engineers, mechanics and drivers had been days away from losing their jobs just seven months earlier.

Brawn GP's surprise success in 2009 was the result of Ross Brawn's ability to design a car that made the most of the sport's new technical regulations. By the time their rivals caught up, Brawn GP had all but sewn up the World Championship.

Ross Brawn achieved so much in Formula 1 with Benetton and Ferrari, but nothing compares to guiding his own team to Constructors and Drivers Championships in 2009.

JENSON BUTTON

There was a time when many in the Formula 1 paddock thought Jenson Button would never make the most of his talents. Having first been given a Formula 1 contract at the age of 20, Button struggled for years to make an impact. Despite his smooth, effortless driving style – under his control, Formula 1 cars seem to glide across the track – and obvious ability, he seemed unable to get the results. His attitude, ability and stomach for the fight were all questioned. Ultimately, he proved the doubters wrong, holding his nerve to become the 2009 World Champion in his ninth season in the sport.

Button's rise through the motor sport ranks was rapid. It took him just two years to go from karting to Formula 1, via a British Championship winning season in Formula Ford and an impressive year in Formula 3. After a successful test with the Prost Formula 1 team, he was signed by Williams' to become the team's second driver for the 2000 season. Big things were expected of the 20 year-old, but he struggled badly and was replaced at the end of the season.

Disappointing spells with Benetton and Renault followed, before Button reignited his faltering career by moving to British American Racing (BAR) in 2003. He enjoyed a strong season in 2004, reaching the podium 10 times to finish third in the World Championship, increasing hopes that he would finally mount a serious title challenge in 2005. Instead, he struggled badly and finished ninth, increasing whispers about his potential to even win races, let alone Championships.

By 2006, with six years in Formula 1 under his belt, Button had yet to win a Grand Prix. It was a statistic that weighed heavy on the man from Frome in Somerset, especially given the faith put in him by new employers Honda. With every passing Grand Prix, the stat just looked worse.

Jenson Button had to work hard to earn his place in the pantheon of Formula 1 legends, winning his first World Championship in his ninth season in the sport.

STATISTICS*

BORN	19th January 1980
NATIONALITY	British
ACTIVE YEARS	2000–present
TEAMS	Williams, Benetton, Renault, BAR, Honda, Brawn GP, McLaren
TOTAL RACES	290
WINS	15
PODIUM FINISHES	50
POLE POSITIONS	8
FIRST WIN	2006 Hungarian Grand Prix
LAST WIN	2012 Brazilian Grand Prix
LAST RACE	–

*Statistics correct as of May 2016

Jenson Button's smooth and technically proficient driving style means he usually performs well in wet conditions.

Jenson Button celebrates winning the 2012 Brazilian Grand Prix. At the time of publication, this was his most recent victory in Formula 1.

Finally, at the 114th time of asking, Button won a race – the 2006 Hungarian Grand Prix. Instead of kick-starting his career, it highlighted his underachievement. To make matters worse, it would be three years before he would win another race.

It didn't help that the Honda cars he was now driving were unreliable and largely uncompetitive. Thankfully, Honda had faith in Button and the team, and stuck with the experienced British driver and his high salary. Then in 2008, their patience ran out and they announced their withdrawal from Formula 1 on financial grounds. Button was left contemplating the end of a career that had spluttered from start to finish.

Luckily, Ross Brawn had a plan. He bought the Honda team, renaming it Brawn GP. Button was offered the chance to continue, albeit it on a vastly reduced salary. He grasped the opportunity with both hands and was rewarded with his first World Championship in 2009.

Having only won one Grand Prix in nine years, he claimed six victories in the first seven races in 2009. He looked like a shoe-in for the World Championship, but as the season wore on and the Brawn car's dominance faded, Button began to look like a man under pressure. To his credit, he didn't crumple under the pressure, and fifth place at the penultimate race of the season in Brazil was enough to secure the title he'd dreamed about winning since he was a youngster.

Button switched to McLaren the following season, where he remains to this day. At 34 years of age, his days in Formula 1 are numbered but he remains one of the sport's most popular drivers. In early 2014 he started his 250th Grand Prix; to date, only four drivers have contested more races.

RUBENS
BARRICHELLO

Rubens Barrichello celebrates wildly after winning the 2009 Italian Grand Prix during his season with Brawn GP. As with much of his career, the Brazilian was forced to play second fiddle to a title-chasing teammate, in this case Jenson Button.

When he retired in 2011, Rubens Barrichello did so as the third highest points scorer in Formula 1 history, and as the man who had contested more races than anyone before or since. He was an integral part of the sport for a year short of two decades – great testament to his consistency, fitness and deep-rooted love of racing.

It could all have been so different, though. In 1994, he was involved in a horrific crash at Imola during practice for the ill-fated San Marino Grand Prix. When he woke up in hospital, friend, mentor and fellow Brazilian driver, Ayrton Senna, was by his bedside; two days later, Senna was dead, himself a victim of a crash at the same track. Barrichello was devastated by the loss of his friend and considered quitting sport for good, only a year after making his debut for Jordan at the 1993 South African Grand Prix.

Barrichello showed great mental strength and tenacity to overcome this setback, a trait that would go on to define his career. He became Formula 1's go-to driver – a team player who was often forced to play second fiddle to Championship-chasing drivers (most notably Michael Schumacher and Jenson Button), but did it with good grace and with none of the histrionics associated with many Formula 1 drivers. Few could argue that he deserved to win the World Championship at some point during his career; in the end, he retired with two near-misses to his name (2002 and 2004).

Barrichello grew up close to the Interlagos track, home of Formula 1 in Brazil. His racing-mad family bought him a Go-Kart aged six, and he never looked back. He won the South American Championship in 1986, aged 14, and a year later came ninth in the World Karting Championships.

Barrichello was often Michael Schumacher's closest rival during his years at Ferrari but he never quite had enough to beat his teammate.

STATISTICS

BORN	23rd May 1972
NATIONALITY	Brazilian
ACTIVE YEARS	1993–2011
TEAMS	Jordan, Stewart, Ferrari, Honda, Brawn GP, Williams
TOTAL RACES	326 (322 starts)
WINS	11
PODIUM FINISHES	68
POLE POSITIONS	14
FIRST WIN	2000 German Grand Prix
LAST WIN	2009 Italian Grand Prix
LAST RACE	2011 Brazilian Grand Prix

Aged 16, Barrichello moved up to Formula Ford, before moving to England to increase his chances of being talent-spotted by a Formula 1 team. His cause was helped when he became the youngest ever driver to win the British Formula 3 Championship in 1991, aged just 19.

After making his Formula 1 debut with the Jordan team in 1993, he enjoyed a number of years scratching round for points, often in poor cars. He moved to the Stewart Ford team in 1997, but things barely improved. There were occasional podium finishes and strong showings on the rare occasion his cars completed a race without some technical fault. All in all, it was a hugely frustrating time for the popular Brazilian.

Moving to the competitive Ferrari team in 2000 saw things improve, and he finally won his first race, the German Grand Prix, the same year. Inside the dominant car of the period, he became a consistent points scorer, though his path towards World Championship success was constantly blocked by teammate Michael Schumacher.

In 2006, he'd finally had enough of shadowing the great German so he joined Jenson Button at Honda. More frustration followed, before Ross Brawn's buyout of the team in 2009 gave him a chance to drive the fastest car on the grid once again. Although he competed well, it was teammate Button who would drive away with the title, much to Barrichello's disappointment.

With his chance of glory gone once again, Williams recruited Barrichello as team leader in 2010. He completed two seasons with the unreliable British team, showing flashes of greatness amidst the disappointments, before calling it a day at the end of 2011. He retired as Formula 1's most experienced driver of all time. Fittingly, his final race was at Interlagos in Brazil, a stone's throw away from where he grew up dreaming of Formula 1 glory.

Barrichello was a popular member of the Formula 1 paddock and retired in 2011 as the most experienced Formula 1 driver of all time.

SEBASTIAN VETTEL

When Michael Schumacher finally retired at the end of the 2012 season with seven World Championships to his name, few thought his record would ever be beaten. Sebastian Vettel, with four titles to his name at just 26 years of age, could yet bypass the mark set by the legendary German.

Comparisons between the two drivers are natural. Vettel is quick and consistent, able to hit the front early on and control a race better than anyone else on the circuit. He's grabbed pole position an amazing 45 times as of April 2014, putting him third on the all-time list of Formula 1 pole-sitters. His haul of 39 wins means that only Schumacher, Alain Prost and Ayrton Senna have more. By the time he retires, he could feasibly have smashed almost all significant Formula 1 records, though he'll have to go some to match Schumacher's amazing haul of 91 Grand Prix wins.

Like Schumacher, Vettel is also ruthless. He gives little away to rivals and when under pressure, is prone to disobeying team orders. He did this most famously at the 2013

Malaysian Grand Prix, where he ignored Red Bull's calls to retain position. Instead he attacked and overtook his teammate, Mark Webber. The latter, already frustrated by perceived favouritism towards his German teammate, was outraged; it was no surprise when he announced his retirement at the end of the season. At Red Bull, there will only ever be one number one.

Like most Formula 1 drivers, Vettel began his racing career in karting, before moving up to the German Formula BMW circuit in 2003 with the support of Red Bull's Driver Development Programme. The following year he won the Championship, winning 18 of 20 races, subsequently moving up to Formula 3 in 2005. It earned him the reserve driver spot with the BMW Sauber Formula 1 team in 2006.

Despite his relentless nature on the track, Sebastian Vettel is known for being laidback and quick-witted off it.

STATISTICS*

BORN	3rd July 1987
NATIONALITY	German
ACTIVE YEARS	2006–present
TEAMS	BMW Sauber, Toro Rosso, Red Bull
TOTAL RACES	161
WINS	42
PODIUM FINISHES	81
POLE POSITIONS	46
FIRST WIN	2008 Italian Grand Prix
LAST WIN	2013 Brazilian Grand Prix
LAST RACE	–

*Statistics correct as of May 2016

Vettel leads teammate Mark Webber at the 2012 Brazilian Grand Prix. It would become a familiar sight during the pair's time together at Red Bull.

Sebastian Vettel was all smiles after coming home sixth at the 2012 Brazilian Grand Prix, a result that secured him a third consecutive World Championship.

Vettel predictably impressed on his debut, finishing eighth in a largely unresponsive car. Red Bull decided to bring him back into the fold, putting him in their second-string Toro Rosso team for the 2007 season. The following year, Vettel gave a taste of what was to come by winning the rain-hit Italian Grand Prix, his first Formula 1 race win. Given that the car was nothing special, the fact that he secured pole and won the race was a remarkable achievement.

He transferred to Red Bull in 2009, winning three times as he pushed Jenson Button all the way in the World Championship. A year later, with Red Bull's talented designer Adrian Newey finally providing him with the best car on the grid, he won his first World Championship at 23 years old, becoming the sport's youngest ever World Champion in the process.

It wasn't all plain sailing, though. Vettel was quick throughout the year but errors cost him points on a number of occasions. He went into the final race of the season 15 points down on Fernando Alonso and seven points behind teammate Mark Webber. Remarkably, Vettel won the decider in Abu Dhabi, with his rivals finishing in midfield. As a result, he snatched the title by a mere four points.

Thus began a period of dominance that had echoes of Michael Schumacher during his years with Ferrari. In 2011, Vettel wrapped up the World Championship with four races to go. He stormed back in the second half of the 2012 season to once again edge out Fernando Alonso and claim a hat-trick of Drivers Championships. Then came 2013, and a run of nine consecutive Grand Prix wins to add a fourth title to his already impressive CV. Few would bet against the talented German securing more World Championships in the years ahead.

FORMULA 1: A NEW ERA

Today, Formula 1 cars are quieter, less powerful but more efficient. The FIA believes these changes, implemented for the 2014 season, will help the sport in the long run.

Daniel Ricciardo became the first driver to be disqualified for breaching Formula 1's new regulations. His Red Bull was fitted with extra fuel sensors at the 2014 Australian Grand Prix.

Formula 1 is no stranger to rule changes – both technical and sporting – and the history of the sport is littered with such tinkering (both successful and unsuccessful). Even so, the changes brought in by the sport's governing body, the FIA, ahead of the 2014 season were among the most radical to date.

Those who keep abreast with Formula 1 rules will have picked up on the most significant changes. The greatest of these is arguably the decision to make engines smaller. Instead of the petrol-guzzling V12 and V8 engines of the past, from 2014 onwards, Formula 1 cars will be fitted with turbocharged, direct-injection 1.6-litre V6 engines. Drivers are allowed to use only five "power-units" (engine, turbo, exhaust, electronics) over the season, with harsh penalties for over-stepping this mark.

There have been major changes to the gears; instead of changing their gear set-up to suit each circuit, drivers have to make do with eight standard gears throughout the season. Given the vast differences in circuits – for example, contrast the twisting street circuit of Monaco with newer circuits blessed with long, fast straights – this could result in some very unpredictable races.

There have also been some aerodynamic changes, a demand for all cars to have a single exhaust at the rear of the car, and a new harder tyre from supplier Pirelli. If that's not enough to cause teams serious headaches, drivers can only use 220 pounds (100 kg) of fuel over an entire race weekend, meaning management of these resources could have a huge outcome on races.

While some of the changes have been criticised – most notably by Ferrari – there's little doubt that they should level the playing field and ensure exciting races.

Ferrari have been vocal opponents of Formula 1's new regulations and have been lobbying hard for a return to bigger engines.

Formula 1 bosses have been delighted by the closeness of races and excitement generated since they brought in new regulations at the start of the 2014 season.

CHAMPIONS 1946–2015

Year	Driver	Team	Nationality
1950	Guiseppi Farina	Alfa Romeo	Italian
1951	Juan Manuel Fangio	Alfa Romeo	Argentinian
1952	Alberto Ascari	Ferrari	Italian
1953	Alberto Ascari	Ferrari	Italian
1954	Juan Manuel Fangio	Maserati/Mercedes	Argentinian
1955	Juan Manuel Fangio	Mercedes	Argentinian
1956	Juan Manuel Fangio	Ferrari	Argentinian
1957	Juan Manuel Fangio	Maserati	Argentinian
1958	Mike Hawthorn	Ferrari	British
1959	Jack Brabham	Cooper	Australian
1960	Jack Brabham	Cooper	Australian
1961	Phil Hill	Ferrari	US
1962	Graham Hill	BRM	British
1963	Jim Clark	Lotus	British
1964	John Surtees	Ferrari	British
1965	Jim Clark	Lotus	British
1966	Jack Brabham	Brabham	Australian
1967	Denny Hulme	Brabham	New Zealander
1968	Graham Hill	Lotus	British
1969	Jackie Stewart	Matra	British
1970	Jochen Rindt	Lotus	Austrian
1971	Jackie Stewart	Tyrrell	British
1972	Emerson Fittipaldi	Lotus	Brazilian
1973	Jackie Stewart	Tyrrell	British
1974	Emerson Fittipaldi	McLaren	Brazilian
1975	Niki Lauda	Ferrari	Austrian
1976	James Hunt	McLaren	British
1977	Niki Lauda	Ferrari	Austrian
1978	Mario Andretti	Lotus	US

1979	Jody Schekter	Ferrari	South African
1980	Alan Jones	Williams	Australian
1981	Nelson Piquet	Brabham	Brazilian
1982	Keke Rosberg	Williams	Finnish
1983	Nelson Piquet	Brabham	Brazilian
1984	Niki Lauda	McLaren	Austrian
1985	Alain Prost	McLaren	French
1986	Alain Prost	McLaren	French
1987	Nelson Piquet	Williams	Brazilian
1988	Ayrton Senna	McLaren	Brazilian
1989	Alain Prost	McLaren	French
1990	Ayrton Senna	McLaren	Brazilian
1991	Ayrton Senna	McLaren	Brazilian
1992	Nigel Mansell	Williams	British
1993	Alain Prost	Williams	French
1994	Michael Schumacher	Benetton	German
1995	Michael Schumacher	Benetton	German
1996	Damon Hill	Williams	British
1997	Jacques Villeneuve	Williams	Canadian
1998	Mika Hakkinen	McLaren	Finnish
1999	Mika Hakkinen	McLaren	Finnish
2000	Michael Schumacher	Ferrari	German
2001	Michael Schumacher	Ferrari	German
2002	Michael Schumacher	Ferrari	German
2003	Michael Schumacher	Ferrari	German
2004	Michael Schumacher	Ferrari	German
2005	Fernando Alonso	Renault	Spanish
2006	Fernando Alonso	Renault	Spanish
2007	Kimi Räikkönen	Ferrari	Finnish
2008	Lewis Hamilton	McLaren	British
2009	Jenson Button	Brawn GP	British
2010	Sebastian Vettel	Red Bull	German
2011	Sebastian Vettel	Red Bull	German
2012	Sebastian Vettel	Red Bull	German
2013	Sebastian Vettel	Red Bull	German
2014	Lewis Hamilton	Mercedes	British
2015	Lewis Hamilton	Mercedes	British

GREAT FORMULA 1 CIRCUITS

CIRCUIT DE MONACO
Where: Monaco, Monte Carlo
Races held: Monaco Grand Prix
Number of races: 62
First used: 1950
Last used: 2015

AUTODROMO NAZIONALE MONZA
Where: Monza, Italy
Races held: Italian Grand Prix
Number of races: 65
First used: 1950
Last used: 2015

SILVERSTONE CIRCUIT
Where: Silverstone, United Kingdom
Races held: British Grand Prix
Number of races: 49
First used: 1950
Last used: 2015

CIRCUIT DE SPA FRANCORCHAMPS
Where: Spa, Belgium
Races held: Belgian Grand Prix
Number of races: 48
First used: 1950
Last used: 2015

NÜRBURGRING
Where: Nürburg, Germany
Races held: German Grand Prix, European Grand Prix, Luxemburg Grand Prix
Number of races: 40
First used: 1951
Last used: 2013

CIRCUIT GILLES VILLENEUVE
Where: Montreal, Canada
Races held: Canadian Grand Prix
Number of races: 36
First used: 1978
Last used: 2015

HOCKENHEIMRING
Where: Hockenheim, Germany
Races held: German Grand Prix
Number of races: 34
First used: 1970
Last used: 2014

AUTODROMO JOSE CARLOS PACE (INTERLAGOS)
Where: Sao Paulo, Brazil
Races held: Brazilian Grand Prix
Number of races: 33
First used: 1973
Last used: 2015

CIRCUIT PARK ZANDVOOORT
Where: Zandvoort, Netherlands
Races held: Dutch Grand Prix
Number of races: 30
First used: 1952
Last used: 1985

HUNGARORING
Where: Budapest, Hungary
Races held: Hungarian Grand Prix
Number of races: 30
First used: 1986
Last used: 2015

AUTODROMO ENZO E DINO FERRARI

Where: Imola, Italy
Races held: Italian Grand Prix, San Marino Grand Prix
Number of races: 27
First used: 1980
Last used: 2006

SUZUKA CIRCUIT

Where: Suzuka, Japan
Races held: Japanese Grand Prix
Number of races: 27
First used: 1987
Last used: 2015

WATKINS GLEN

Where: Watkins Glen, New York, USA
Races held: United States Grand Prix
Number of races: 20
First used: 1961
Last used: 1980

KYALAMI

Where: Midrand, South Africa
Races held: South African Grand Prix
Number of races: 20
First used: 1967
Last used: 1993

INDIANAPOLIS MOTOR SPEEDWAY

Where: Indianapolis, USA
Races held: United States Grand Prix
Number of races: 19
First used: 1950
Last used: 2007

SEPANG INTERNATIONAL CIRCUIT

Where: Kuala Lumpur, Malaysia
Races held: Malaysian Grand Prix
Number of races: 17
First used: 1999
Last used: 2015

RED BULL RING (A1-RING)

Where: Zeltweg, Austria
Races held: Austrian Grand Prix
Number of races: 27
First used: 1970
Last used: 2015

CIRCUIT DE CATALUNYA

Where: Mentmelo, Spain
Races held: Spanish Grand Prix
Number of races: 25
First used: 1991
Last used: 2015

AUTODROMO JUAN U OSCAR GALVEZ

Where: Buenos Aries, Argentina
Races held: Argentinian Grand Prix
Number of races: 20
First used: 1953
Last used: 1998

CIRCUIT DE NEVERS MAGNY-COURS

Where: Nevers, France
Races held: French Grand Prix
Number of races: 18
First used: 1991
Last used: 2008

ALBERT PARK

Where: Melbourne, Australia
Races held: Australian Grand Prix
Number of races: 21
First used: 1996
Last used: 2015

AUTODROMO HERMANOS RODRIGUEZ

Where: Mexico City, Mexico
Races held: Mexican Grand Prix
Number of races: 15
First used: 1963
Last used: 1992

Statistics correct as of December 2015